THE SAMUEL AND ALTHEA STROUM LECTURES
IN JEWISH STUDIES

Recent Archaeological Discoveries and Biblical Research

WILLIAM G. DEVER

UNIVERSITY OF WASHINGTON PRESS

Seattle and London

Library of Congress Cataloging-in-Publication Data
Dever, William G.
Recent archaeological discoveries and biblical research
(Samuel and Althea Stroum lectures in Jewish studies)
Bibliography: p.
Includes index.
1. Bible. O.T.—Antiquities. 2. Palestine—
Antiquities. 3. Excavations (Archaeology)—Palestine.
I. Title. II. Series.
BS621.D49 1989 88–34386
ISBN 0-295-96588-6

The paper used in this publication meets the minimum requirements of American National Standard for Information Sciences — Permanence of Paper for Printed Library Materials, ANSI Z39.48–1984.

∞

THE SAMUEL AND ALTHEA STROUM LECTURES
IN JEWISH STUDIES

Samuel Stroum, businessman, community leader, and philanthropist, by a major gift to the Jewish Federation of Greater Seattle, established the Samuel and Althea Stroum Philanthropic Fund.

In recognition of Mr. and Mrs. Stroum's deep interest in Jewish history and culture, the Board of Directors of the Jewish Federation of Greater Seattle, in cooperation with the Jewish Studies Program of the Henry M. Jackson School of International Studies at the University of Washington, established an annual lectureship at the University of Washington known as the Samuel and Althea Stroum Lectureship in Jewish Studies. This lectureship makes it possible to bring to the area outstanding scholars and interpreters of Jewish thought, thus promoting a deeper understanding of Jewish history, religion, and culture. Such understanding can lead to an enhanced appreciation of the Jewish contributions to the historical and cultural traditions that have shaped the American nation.

The terms of the gift also provide for the publication from time to time of the lectures or other appropriate materials resulting from or related to the lectures.

Contents

Acknowledgments

I wish to express my deep gratitude to Mr. Samuel N. and Mrs. Althea Stroum of Seattle, whose generosity made this lectureship possible, and whose warm hospitality helped to make my visit to the University of Washington a memorable occasion. I am also indebted to Professor Jere Bacharach, who first suggested my name to the selection committee, to Mrs. Dorothy Becker, who handled all the practical arrangements with admirable efficiency; and to Naomi Pascal and the staff of the University of Washington Press, who were a delight to work with. The manuscript for this book was typed by my wife Norma, who accompanied me to Seattle in April 1985.

Whatever I may have to offer in these lectures I owe to my two teachers and mentors, the late professors G. Ernest Wright of Harvard University and Nelson Glueck of the Hebrew Union College–Jewish Institute of Religion, whose two archaeological institutes in Jerusalem (HUC-JIR and ASOR) I later served as director from 1968 to 1975. Much of the first-hand information on excavations in Israel I owe to my Israeli colleagues, who have generously made unpublished material available to me. I wish also to thank several of my doctoral students in archaeology at the University of Arizona, who made valuable suggestions in seminars where some of these ideas were first tried out. Finally, I am grateful to my friend and former colleague in Biblical studies at Arizona, Professor Peter Machinist, who constantly encourages me to relate archaeology to Biblical studies. Professor Machinist made many constructive criticisms of this manuscript, but of course he is not to be held accountable for the peculiarities of my personal views.

I am a Syro-Palestinian archaeologist, but I began, like most of my generation, as a seminarian and clergyman. Although I retain a keen interest in Biblical studies, I cannot claim to make any original contribution

ix

in these lectures; indeed, I only hope that my assessment of the current situation in Biblical studies represents a consensus among specialists. Since these were intended as popular lectures, primarily to acquaint the layman interested in the Bible with some of the latest methods and results of archaeology in the Holy Land, I have presented them here substantially as delivered. The student may find, however, sufficient documentation in the Notes to pursue certain topics further. If these preliminary thoughts serve to stimulate the dialogue between archaeologists and students of the Hebrew Bible, I shall have achieved my aim.

WILLIAM G. DEVER
Tucson, Arizona
Christmas/Hannukah 1985

I

ARTIFACTS, ECOFACTS, AND TEXTUAL FACTS

*How Archaeology Today
Can Illuminate
the World of the Bible*

"ARCHAEOLOGY" and "Bible"—two simple household terms in America, often used together, understood by everyone. But are they understood properly? If so, why are both subject to such controversy? And what can archaeology contribute to our understanding of the Bible?

These are the problems I wish to address in these lectures, first by looking at the nature and recent development of both archaeology and Biblical studies; then by laying the groundwork for a new and more productive relationship between these two disciplines; and then by taking as case studies three eras in ancient Israelite history, to show by means of recent discoveries how archaeology, properly coupled with textual study, can illuminate the life and times of ancient Israel.

I want to stress at the beginning how selective we must be, given the flood of new light from archaeological discoveries; our evidence will be drawn largely from excavations and surveys done in Israel in the last ten years, many still unpublished. We shall further restrict our inquiry to the Old Testament (more properly, the "Hebrew Bible"), since New Testament archaeology, or the archaeology of Late Antiquity, is best considered a separate discipline, still in its infancy (and also beyond my specialization).

The Hebrew Bible as a Source of History

At the outset we must define the two referents of our discussion: *archaeology* and *Bible*; then we may chart the development of modern archaeology as a discipline, with special reference to Biblical studies. Let us begin by asking to what extent the Hebrew Bible can be used as a source book for writing history. Underlying this question is an assumption that I hope to demonstrate before we are through, namely that archaeology can comment only on historical problems, not theological ones—and indeed only on certain kinds of historical problems.

The Bible is commonly referred to as a book, or even "the Book," as both Jewish and Christian communities have dictated by regarding it as authoritative Scripture. But the Bible is many books, not simply because tradition and canon divide it into twenty-four (or thirty-nine) separate volumes, but primarily because it contains a bewildering array of types of literature. Only a few of these, comprising a minority of Biblical texts, can legitimately be used by the modern historian for writing a critical history of ancient Israel.

Nineteenth- and twentieth-century literary criticism and other types of criticism have shown that the Hebrew Bible is a composite of such diverse genres as myths, folktales, epic, prose and poetic narratives, court annals, nationalist propaganda, historical novellas, biography, genealogies, cult legend and liturgical formulae, songs and psalms, private prayers, legal *corpora*, oracle and prophecy, homily and didactic material, belles lettres, erotic poetry, apocalyptic, and still other literary forms.[1] Which of these, if any, can be utilized by the modern historian or student of the Bible who wants to know what things were really like in the past? And which can archaeology illustrate?

It is relatively easy to illustrate, and therefore to eliminate as history, several of the literary genres just listed. For example, the myths of Genesis 1–11, comprising the "primeval history," which deal with the creation, the flood, and the distant origins of the family of man, can be read today as deeply moving literature, with profound moral implications. They inform us about the thought-world of ancient Israel, but they can hardly be read in the literal or modern sense as history. The legitimate archaeologist (in contrast to the "raider of the lost ark") will therefore not attempt to date the creation, or set out to locate the Garden of Eden and excavate the bones of Adam and Eve, or establish flood levels and dig up the timbers of Noah's ark. These are memorable, indeed universal tales, whose primary purpose and place in the Hebrew Bible is theological, not historical; they are clearly intended as the prolegomenon to the story that follows, of "God's saving acts" on behalf of his chosen people Israel.[2]

When we come to the later portions of Genesis and to the book of Exodus—the story of the Patriarchal and Mosaic eras—there are obviously more properly historical data, such as connected narrative supported by numerous details that ring true in the light of what we actually know of the second millennium B.C. in Syria-Palestine and Egypt. But even in this material there persist elements of legend—heroic figures who live for hundreds of years, casual appearances of angels, and miracles of all kinds—not to mention anachronisms of style that date the writing to a period centuries after the events they purport to record. The result, as we shall see, is that after a century of modern research neither Biblical scholars nor archaeologists have been able to document as historical any of the events, much less the personalities, of the Mosaic era.[3]

On the other hand, for the emergence of Israel in Canaan in the twelfth to eleventh centuries B.C., we have in the books of Joshua and Judges much more contemporary records and eye-witness accounts, especially in archaic poems such as the "Song of Deborah," cultic material still close to its Canaanite sources, territorial and tribal lists, and so forth. Yet even here it must be stressed that Joshua and Judges give differing accounts of the so-called conquest and settlement of Canaan—accounts that cannot be readily reconciled, as we shall see, especially when newer archaeological evidence is considered. Which is true? Both? Neither? How shall we choose? And what role should archaeological evidence play in the decision?

Scholars have long recognized that only with the United Monarchy, beginning in the early tenth century B.C., do we have reasonably reliable historical sources, such as the "Court History of David" contained in the books of Samuel. Following that, in the Divided Monarchy, we have in the books of Kings (and, to a lesser degree, in the parallel accounts in Chronicles) similarly reliable sources, which can now be checked against contemporary records from Egypt and especially from Assyria and Babylonia. Finally, the prophetic books of the eighth through sixth centuries B.C. and the wisdom literature are full of invaluable social and political commentary and also contain many vivid, detailed descriptions of everyday life in ancient Israel.[4] Yet even these present certain problems of interpretation.

Whatever degree of historical reliability we encounter in the various literary genres of the Hebrew Bible, it is evident that all require careful critical interpretation before they can be used by the historian of ancient Israel. The Bible cannot simply be read at face value as history; nor, of course, can any other ancient text be so read. We must begin by acknowledging that our task is made difficult, some would say impossible, by problems in the nature of the literary sources—even the properly historical sources—and the written tradition in which they have been handed down to us.[5]

First, there is in the Bible no real historiography in the modern sense; indeed, the word "history" does not appear once in the Hebrew Bible. The Biblical writers rarely claim to base themselves solely on factual records, to be totally objective, or to cover the whole story. They are concerned not with the question, "What really happened?" but with the larger question, "What does it mean?" For them and for their original readers, the Bible is "His story," the interpretation of certain happenings as seen through the eyes of faith, the story of the saving acts of God on behalf of his people. To be sure, the Bible is historical in the sense that it contains an account of particular peoples and occurrences at particular places and times, and in this respect it contrasts sharply with some of the mythological literatures of other ancient religions. But concrete events are important in the Bible only as they illustrate God's actions and their consequences for people here and now. The modern notion of a disinterested secular history would have been inconceivable to Biblical writers, nor would they have been interested in it had they conceived of it.[6]

Second, because of the radical theological nature of even the descriptive, historical portions of the Bible, the writers were highly selective about what they included. They simply do not tell us many things that we "moderns" wish to know. For instance, the eighth-century B.C. writers portray on a grand scale the dramatic public actions of great kings, priests, reformers, and prophets, but they tell us next to nothing about the daily life of the average Israelite or Judean. The Bible is concerned with *political* history, not social or economic history, much less individual history (except for biographies of certain "great men"). Nowhere in the Bible do we have more than a passing hint about what most people looked like, what they wore or ate, what their houses and furniture were like, what went on in the streets and plazas of the average town, how agriculture and trade were conducted, how people wrote and kept records, how they went about their daily chores and entertained themselves, how long they lived and what they died of, or how they were buried. These are precisely the details that archaeology can supply. The Bible describes pub lic life and the "world of the spirit"; archaeology fills in a knowledge of everyday life and culture. Both are necessary if we are to comprehend ancient Israel in its full variety and vitality.

A third difficulty we encounter in trying to read the Bible as history is that virtually all of its accounts, in their present written form, are later than the events they describe, often centuries later. Thus the supposedly "Mosaic" legislation of Deuteronomy stems from a school of reformers in the eighth and seventh centuries B.C., at the earliest. The idealistic descriptions of the priesthood and the sacrificial system in Leviticus, supposedly set in the period of the Judges and the Monarchy, are the product of the priestly school during the Exile and the return, when the Temple and its establishment had long since been destroyed. There is, to be sure, genuinely archaic material in all the above and other Pentateuchal sources. But modern scholarship has shown beyond doubt that it is encrusted with much later tradition; and, above all, that it is heavily edited by the late redactors who assembled the Hebrew Bible in its present form, the last portions dating not before the second century B.C. Here the attraction of archaeology is simply that it offers the possibility of getting beyond these late, reworked sources to contemporary, firsthand records and other remains that may, under the right circumstances, illuminate certain events directly.

Finally, not only are the historical texts in the Bible late, but they are "elitist." They were written by and for the upper classes, and they were interpreted, preserved, and transmitted by them. Ultimately, the Bible as we have it is almost entirely a product of the royal court and the priestly establishment in Jerusalem. Even the classical prophets—usually thought of as populist reformers who had risen from among the people—were cult officials; and without exception their biographies and collected works, as we have them, were reworked and passed on by literary schools bearing their names.

For all its "democratic" touches, in its portrayal of religion the Bible is largely elitist; it presents a highly idealized, spiritualized picture of normative religion—what people should have believed and practiced in the name of Yahweh. Fortunately, not all dissenting views were suppressed, so that in the Biblical literature we also have a glimpse of the counter-culture, of folk religion, and of unorthodox schools of thought that did not survive in the long run. Archaeology is uniquely equipped to view this other side of the coin, and thus supply a corroborative picture (see chapter 4).

Even supposing there were agreement concerning the nature of the Bible's literary sources, there would remain numerous problems in the transmission of the text. The Massoretic manuscripts of the Hebrew Bible, upon which all our modern printed Bibles are based, are called collectively the *textus receptus*—the "received text." But how did we receive it, in what form and by what means? How old is this text, how accurately does it reflect the lost originals, and thus how close can it be to the truth of what really happened? It must always be remembered that the Massoretic text is medieval (ca. ninth century A.D.); that even our oldest fragments of manuscripts date back only to the Greco-Roman era (as the Dead Sea Scrolls); and that, despite fanatically careful copying by scribes over the centuries, some texts in the Hebrew Bible have become so corrupt that they simply cannot be translated with any certainty.[7] We must constantly keep in mind the fact that the Bible is a fragment of a very ancient literature in a dead language, until the discoveries of modern archaeology, the sole relic of a long-lost culture, and the product of an ancient oriental conceptual world totally foreign to most of us. We must therefore beware of "modernizing" the Bible. Believers who read only modern English translations of the Biblical text, often unaware of the long transmission process, speak of the "plain meaning" of Scripture. If there were any such thing, we would have none of the violent controversies that have always surrounded the interpretation of the Bible—beginning already in antiquity and continuing through every popular and scholarly school, both Jewish and Christian, to this very moment.[8] Here again, the attraction of archaeology is its promise to render many difficult passages more intelligible either by finding parallel texts that may explain enigmatic phrases (as the Ugaritic texts have done brilliantly), or by putting Biblical texts back into their original context so as to restore their full meaning. The latter promise will be discussed below.

In the light of what I have just said about the nature of the Biblical texts themselves and the way they have come down to us, I am going to put forward a novel and perhaps bold approach to the Hebrew Bible, one drawn from archaeology. I suggest that it will be helpful to compare the Bible to other relics from antiquity—indeed, to view it, in archaeological terminology, as a "curated artifact."

It ought not be controversial to state that the Bible is an artifact—that is, something fabricated by the human brain and hand. It is a shaped material object that, like any other artifact, reflects the human thought and behavior that produced it. It is thus a symbol, the visible reality that points to an invisible reality beyond it, as the catechism has it, the "outward sign of an inward truth." This concept of the Bible as an artifact is not as revolutionary as it may first seem, nor does it necessarily detract from it as Scripture (that is, a divine rather than a merely human document). It simply highlights what most of us instinctively know, that the Bible, like all great literature, is best read not in a literalistic but in a symbolic sense. More than other language, this "god-language" is symbolic—it is only an approximation of ultimate reality. The Bible is not the "word of God" in itself (as the Fundamentalist doctrine of verbal inspiration holds), but rather may become the "word of God" insofar as it points beyond itself, to the God who stands above all human description.

I wish to regard the Bible here as an artifact (although not simply that) so that I may show how the problems of its interpretation are remarkably similar to those of archaeological artifacts. If I am correct, then the two disciplines of our present inquiry are organically related—more so than earlier Biblical archaeologists thought, but for different reasons.

Think of it this way. The study of all artifacts, including texts, is subject to certain restrictions. To begin with, artifacts do not come conveniently labelled as to what they are, or what they mean; in theory, the message is there, but it is in a code that we must decipher. That is as true of a Biblical passage as of an ancient object. Furthermore, we often speak of both texts and archaeological objects as "data" for reconstructing the past. They may constitute evidence, direct or indirect, but they become true data—that is, meaningful facts—only as they are interpreted. Meaning may be inherent in isolated facts, but it can materialize only as we place those facts in the larger framework of both their original context and our own current concerns. For example, a textual passage may have a number of individual words, all of which (in theory) we should be able to read and translate; or a pot has a familiar shape and decoration, whose development we can chart. But we are still far from knowing what these observable phenomena meant to those who wrote and made these things, and what can they mean to us today. With a text, as with a pot, a proper interpretation is only possible as we succeed in balancing two apparently opposite qualities. We must have the empathy that is fundamental to any inquiry, in order to bring us close enough to understand; but at the same time we must be disinterested, keeping the distance necessary to put things in perspective. Sometimes it is assumed that the interpretation of texts is "objective" and therefore superior, while that of artifacts is "subjective" and therefore inferior. Yet all profound and true interpretation involves *both*—that is, critical evaluation plus intuition. This is true of all archaeological argument—which is why it can never be truly scientific in the narrow sense—but it is more true of the historical and religious texts of the Bible, which are a unique blend of facts and faith, and require the same of us before we can hope to understand them at all. Finally, even the best interpretation is only an educated guess. We can never know exactly what an ancient text meant to its author or its original readers, a pot to its maker and user, because we cannot get back into their world, much less "into their heads." We can never really know what it was like in the past; and, ironically, the sooner we get rid of that illusion, the sooner we shall see at least part of the picture clearly.[9]

For the archaeologist, an artifact may be found either *in situ*, in which case the context should yield clues to its original use, or in secondary context, in which case we say that it is "curated." By that we mean essentially that the artifact has been deliberately preserved, repaired and/or altered, and usually put to a somewhat different use from that for which it was originally intended.[10] (Even if the old artifact functioned in the same general way, its use in a later community gives it a slightly different meaning.) In the case of such a curated artifact, the archaeologist must try to discover both what the object was, as well as what it has later become. For example, a broken pot may become an oil lamp, a discarded limestone mortar a door socket, a fragment of an inscribed stone a building block.

In more extreme cases, a ruined temple may be partially reused as a stable. Which is the true use, the original or the secondary? The answer is obviously both.

On analogy, the Bible is also a curated artifact. It was never discovered *in situ*, in its original context in the soil of ancient Palestine, because it was never lost. It is unique in being the sole surviving relic of the ancient Near East that has been continuously preserved, refurbished, and transmitted by a living community, instead of having been dug up by archaeologists centuries after its discard. Thus the Bible is not simply what it was for its original readers in ancient Israel, but that plus what it has become over the long centuries of its continual reworking and reinterpretation by both the Jewish and Christian communities, in the constantly changing situations of religious life all around the world. The Hebrew Bible is a venerable artifact, polished and burnished by loving use over thirty centuries until it has taken on a rich, subtle patina that cannot be stripped away without damaging what is beneath.

This special character of the Bible is a handicap to the historian, for it means that if we are confined to the text we cannot expect simply to penetrate behind the tradition and get directly to the events that gave rise to it. In its present form as a "curated artifact," it more readily reveals its secondary use in late antiquity and in medieval and modern times as a sourcebook of theology and morality—especially in the Western world. It is evident that we can recover its original use as historical commentary in the oriental world of the first millennium B.C. only if we can put the text back into its original context. And that is precisely the contribution that archaeology can make. It alone has the potential of turning up evidence "frozen in time," not subject to later interpretation. Archaeology offers a contemporary but more objective account of conditions and events in the ancient world. Tradition, by its very nature, colors the original events by filtering them through experience and faith. But archaeology allows us a fleeting glimpse of past reality without some of the filters, so that it may be seen in its true colors.

Archaeology as a Parallel Way of Viewing the Past

The archaeology of ancient Palestine has always been conceived, at least in America, as being intimately bound up with Biblical studies. Although I shall here attempt to redefine this relationship, I do accept that it is legitimate and, indeed, fundamental. The two separate but parallel disciplines begin at the same point and with similar data—one largely with textual data and the other largely with artifactual data—which, as we have seen, pose similar problems of interpretation. It is also true that both disciplines have the same goal at the descriptive-historical level (if not at the normative-explanatory level): the fullest possible reconstruction of past life styles and even, if possible, thought forms. Finally, the two disciplines may be called parallel inasmuch as they never converge—despite our expectations.

The story of the development of these complementary and sometimes competing schools of research has never been fully told. There is no space to tell it here, but it is essential to understand that it resembles the merging and separating of two tributaries of the same great river.

The earliest—and until recently the dominant—stream I shall here refer to as "Biblical archaeology." By this I mean the pursuit of the archaeology of the Levant, which is conceived by the pursuers primarily as "the Holy Land." It is an endeavor whose methods and objectives derive largely from problems of Biblical history.[11] Biblical archaeology may be said to have begun with Edward Robinson, rightly considered the founder of modern Palestinology. Robinson was an American Biblical scholar and seminary professor, who during topographical research on journeys in 1838 and again in 1851 rediscovered more than two hundred long lost Biblical sites, even before the birth of modern archaeology, by utilizing Arabic place-names. Robinson laid the groundwork for all modern historical geography and archaeology and, furthermore, permanently fixed the attention of the American scholarly and lay public on the potential of scientific exploration in the Holy Land for illuminating problems of Biblical interpretation. In Robinson's identifications of Biblical sites that countless pilgrims over the centuries had missed or had mislocated, it was precisely the combination of his rigorous scholarship and his being steeped in Biblical languages and lore that brought success. As the great German scholar Albrecht Alt declared on the centennial of Robinson's first journey, "In Robinson's footnotes are forever buried the errors of many generations."[12]

But it was not until much later that Americans undertook actual fieldwork in Palestine. Systematic excavation of specific sites did not begin in Palestine until the work of the eccentric British scholar Sir William Flinders Petrie, at Tell el-Ḥesi (possibly Biblical Eglon) in 1890. Meanwhile, Americans had begun to feel left out as Europeans pushed forward in the rapid exploration and recovery of spectacular monuments and written records in Bible lands from Egypt to Mesopotamia in the mid- to late nineteenth century. In 1870, the American Palestine Exploration Society was launched, with a statement of purpose modelled on that of the British Palestine Exploration Society begun five years earlier, except that the American statement closed with the words "[a society] for the illustration and *defense* of the Bible"—as we shall see, a significantly American departure. In the first volume of the society's *Memoirs* a clarion call for American involvement in fieldwork was issued, combining the Biblical motivation with patriotism: the society existed "to call Americans to their duty in a field where their own countrymen [a reference to Robinson] were pioneers, and where American scholarship and enterprise have won such distinguished merit. If of late we have suffered France, Germany, and especially England to lead us, their success should stimulate us to an honorable rivalry for a precedence that was once fairly American."[13]

Thirty years later, in 1900, a start was finally made when the Archaeological Institute of America, the American Oriental Society, and the Society for Biblical Literature and Exegesis (again note the combination) founded the American School of Oriental Research in Jerusalem. This organization would finally focus American aspirations in archaeology, with a distinctive flair in both fieldwork and scholarship—particularly under the leadership of its most prominent director, William Foxwell Albright.[14]

It was really Albright who deserves credit for the establishment, albeit a brief one, of Biblical archaeology as a respectable academic discipline.

The child of American missionary parents, Albright became the most distinguished Orientalist this country has ever produced. His bibliography of over twelve hundred items is a sizeable book itself. Having mastered Assyriology, Egyptology, and ancient Near Eastern history, he moved on to Northwest Semitic philology and Palestinian archaeology, where he was soon the acknowledged master. For a generation he dominated American Old Testament studies, first as director of the famed American School of Oriental Research in Jerusalem (now named for him) in the 1920s and 1930s, then until 1958 as professor at the Johns Hopkins University, where he turned out more than fifty Ph.D.s.

One of the chief distinguishing marks of the "Albright school," whose overriding influence has only recently been challenged, was its insistence that our branch of archaeology was largely an adjunct of Biblical studies, and should therefore be defined as a special kind of research into the material culture and epigraphic discoveries of all the lands of the Bible. In one of Albright's much-quoted definitions he declared, "The term 'biblical archaeology' may be restricted to Palestine, or it may be extended to include anything that illustrates the Bible, however superficially. Accordingly, I shall use the term 'biblical archaeology' here to refer to all Biblical lands—from India to Spain, and from southern Russia to Southern Arabia—and to the whole history of those lands from about 10,000 B.C., or even earlier, to the present time."[15] In practice, the excavations sponsored by the Jerusalem school under Albright in the 1920s and 1930s—the heyday of fieldwork for this particular school—were all carried out at Old Testament sites, directed by Biblical scholars, and funded by seminaries and church-affiliated schools.

The agenda in these formative years of Biblical archaeology was fixed by Albright's own primary research concerns, which remained remarkably consistent over a fifty-year career. In retrospect, it is clear that Albright was largely reacting against the still prevailing extremes of nineteenth-century European-style literary criticism. This had fragmented the Hebrew Bible into late, heavily edited documents, or literary sources, and had thus cast doubt upon the historicity of much that it contained. Lest we take this as simply another esoteric scholarly debate, we must recall that it was precisely this development in Biblical studies that had precipitated the early twentieth-century Fundamentalist-Modernist controversy that split every major Protestant denomination in America, provoked a crisis in Roman Catholic life, and has shaped much of American religious life ever since. Particularly at issue was the primeval and pre-Monarchical history in the Pentateuch—that is, the Biblical account of the Patriarchal and Mosaic eras. But the "documentary hypothesis," as it came to be called, also regarded much of Joshua-Judges, and even Samuel-Kings, as late and unreliable source material. Above all, this school held that Israelite monotheism was a product of the post-Exilic period, which the Biblical writers had simply projected back into an imaginary Mosaic era. If that were true, the account in the Hebrew Bible of Israel's historical and religious development was a purely literary fancy. To put it another way, the Bible contained little real history about Israel's earliest periods; all that was possible to recover was a history of the literature about the religion of Israel. As one outraged Evangelical put it, this view would make the Bible "nothing more than a pious fraud."

Although it was pioneered in Europe, the new literary or "higher" criticism of the Bible (as distinguished from "lower" or textual criticism) burst upon the American religious scene in the late nineteenth and early twentieth century with a vengeance. It was not perceived as posing quite the same threat to either Jewish or Roman Catholic religious life, since both depended more on later tradition, ethnicity, and piety, and less on the Bible as the primary authority. For Protestantism, however, higher criticism struck a mortal blow to the very heart: the doctrine of verbal inspiration, the concept of the Bible as "the word of God." As early as the turn of the century, a few Protestant Evangelicals had come up with the notion that archaeology would come to their aid by proving the historicity of Biblical personalities and events. One of the earliest works was A. H. Sayce's 1894 *Higher Criticism and the Monuments* and his later *Monumental Facts and Higher Critical Fancies*. A prominent member of this school was Melvin G. Kyle, an editor of the 1906 Evangelical multi-volume series *The Fundamentals* (which really gave its name to the Fundamentalist-Modernist controversy) and later associate director of Albright's own excavations at Tell Beit Mirsim (1926–32). Kyle produced several books typical of this genre, now only historical curiosities but once influential: *The*

Deciding Voice of the Monuments in Biblical Criticism (1912), and *The Problem of the Pentateuch: A New Solution by Archaeological Methods* (1920). By the 1930s there was a considerable literature in America in this vein. Thus in W. W. Prescott's *The Spade and the Bible: Archaeological Discoveries Support the Old Book* (1933), Newton is quoted as declaring "Not a ruined city has been opened up that has given any comfort to unbelieving critics or evolutionists. Every find of archaeologists in Bible lands has gone to confirm Scripture and confound its enemies. . . . Not since Christ ascended back to heaven have there been so many scientific proofs that God's word is truth."[16]

Here it must be stressed that the contribution of Albright was to elevate the amateur Palestinian archaeology of that early period to the level of a budding science, and at the same time to advance beyond the crude and naïve Biblicism of the works cited above to a sound, historically and critically based discipline of Biblical history. The result was a highly respected and widely influential school that represents Biblical archaeology at its finest—in contrast to the Biblical archaeology that still dominates the popular scene in America, with its notion that archaeology's chief business is to "prove" the Bible. Albright is not to blame, of course, for the popular distortion of his views; but his conservatism did invite misinterpretation. Consider, for instance, this statement in 1935, typical of his position, and repeated in one form or another even in his last works: "Archaeological research in Palestine and neighboring lands during the past century has completely transformed our knowledge of the historical and literary background of the Bible. It no longer appears as an absolutely isolated monument of the past, as a phenomenon without relation to its environment. The excessive skepticism shown toward the Bible by important historical schools of the eighteenth and nineteenth century . . . has been progressively discredited. Discovery after discovery has brought increased recognition of the value of the Bible as a source of history."[17] This is certainly a far cry from Fundamentalism. We should note the rather modest claims here, and contrast this statement with that of Newton quoted above. But how shall we then assess "Biblical archaeology" of the Albrightian style?

The last, fullest, and most controversial expression of American-style Biblical archaeology was seen in the work of the late George Ernest Wright, my own teacher. From the 1950s to the 1970s, Wright was at once a prominent churchman and principal spokesman of the Neo-Orthodox Biblical Theology movement, and at the same time the protégé of Albright, who became in turn the leading American Palestinian archaeologist. When Wright left McCormick Theological Seminary in 1958 to become Parkman Professor of Divinity at Harvard, he was able not only to continue and expand his excavations at Shechem—the parade example of modern Biblical archaeology—but also to train a new generation of younger American Palestinian archaeologists who today dominate the field.

In 1952, Wright published a small book that became a classic of American Biblical theology, *God Who Acts: Biblical Theology as Recital*. Wright was reacting against the postwar conception of the Bible, especially in European circles, as mythology that had to be "demythologized." Therefore he stressed rather the historical basis of Biblical religion, which he conceived as the confessional recitation of the *magnalia Dei*, the "mighty acts of God" on behalf of his people. Wright declared that "to participate in Biblical faith means that we must indeed take history seriously as the primary data of the faith." He went even further to say that "in Biblical faith everything depends upon whether the central events [i.e., the deliverance from Egypt, the giving of the Law at Sinai, the conquest of Canaan] actually occurred." Finally, Wright invoked both modern historical and literary criticism and recent progress in archaeology to defend what he called "a greater confidence in the basic reliability of Biblical history."[18]

In the late 1950s Wright, who was already a well-known Palestinian archaeologist in America, came to international attention, especially with his excavations at Biblical Shechem (1956). In 1957 he published his semi-popular book *Biblical Archaeology* almost at the same time as another pivotal work of the Albright school appeared, John Bright's textbook, *The History of Israel* (1958). The reaction in Europe, especially in Germany, was extremely negative and quickly polarized the discussion, largely because of the positivist outlook of the Albrightian approach to early Israelite history. But there were also deep suspicions that the distinctively American combination of archaeology and Biblical studies was dangerously close to fundamentalism. Ten years later a similar reaction greeted Wright's publication of his fieldwork, *Shechem: The Biography of a Biblical City* (1965).

Several of the results of this 1950s controversy overflowed into the popular literature in a rather revealing manner. In 1956 the German journalist Werner Keller seized upon the issues in a book that soon became a runaway best seller and is still widely read and quoted, *The Bible as History: A Confirmation of the Book of Books*. Few have noted that the German original is titled *Und die Bibel hat doch Recht*—roughly translated "The Bible Was Right After All." The well-known American rabbi-explorer-archaeologist, Nelson Glueck, another protégé of Albright, became involved in this controversy when he was attacked by some of his colleagues for entitling his MB I explorations in southern Israel "The Age of Abraham in the Negev." Wright came to his defense in an article in the *Biblical Archaeologist* that became a minor classic, "Is Nelson Glueck's Aim to Prove the Bible?" Wright said no, but suspicions lingered.[19]

Wright's views on Biblical archaeology are of particular significance, for despite his claim that the discipline had been founded earlier by his teacher Albright, many would credit Wright himself with the specific combination of Biblical theology and Palestinian archaeology. (Albright had merely stressed the latter's contribution to Biblical history.) Wright's definition of Biblical archaeology in his first survey of Palestinian archaeology under that rubric in 1947 was repeated almost verbatim in his 1957 textbook:

Biblical archaeology is a special "armchair" variety of general archaeology. The Biblical archaeologist may or may not be an excavator himself, but he studies the discoveries of the excavations in order to glean from them every fact that throws a direct, indirect or even diffused light upon the Bible. He must be intelligently concerned with stratigraphy and typology, upon which the methodology of modern archaeology rests. . . . Yet his chief concern is not with methods or pots or weapons in themselves alone. His central and absorbing interest is the understanding and exposition of the Scriptures.[20]

Here one should note the frank recognition by a founder of Biblical archaeology that it is both an amateur enterprise (not an independent professional or academic discipline) and an inquiry that has as its main objective questions of Biblical faith and practice—not archaeology. It would be helpful had other practitioners of the art been as precise and candid as Wright.

Another ten years or so later, in his last survey of the field, "Biblical Archaeology Today" (1969), Wright spelled out in more detail his rationale, arguing that Biblical archaeology is an organic branch of Biblical and theological studies. In fact, as Wright develops his essay, it becomes clear that for him these two fields of inquiry are not only related but almost identical. Although he admits that it may seem surprising, Wright deals deliberately (and almost exclusively) with "the history of Israel, comparative literature, and comparative religion." He concludes, "Perhaps what I have said in this paper does not sound like archaeology. Yet to me all of it falls under the scope of *Biblical* archaeology."[21] One could scarcely ask for better confirmation of the critique that I shall now offer.

I would contend that the Biblical archaeology movement in its classic form, which dominated the American scene up until about 1970, was really not so much a branch of Near Eastern archaeology as it was a subsidiary of Biblical and theological studies, indeed a chapter in the history of American religious life. *This school drew its agenda not from archaeology but from problems of Biblical research.* Its method stressed academic training in Biblical languages and history plus practical field experience, not graduate professional work in archaeology, anthropology, and science. Its practitioners were all Biblical scholars and teachers, almost without exception "amateur" in the sense of being part-time archaeologists (and proud of it!). The sites chosen for excavation were Biblical, and the support came from seminaries and church-affiliated institutions and individuals. The principal strategies—stratigraphy and ceramic chronology (which were indeed developed to a very high level of technical competence)—focussed primarily on recovering not economic or social history, but a political history of pivotal individuals and public events. Particularly important were fortification systems, public buildings, pottery sequences, and especially destruction layers—all of which, it was thought, could be related directly to Biblical chronology and the supposedly historical accounts of the Biblical literature.[22] We shall see presently that even in these earliest formulations there were sown the seeds of the movement's dissolution.

I began this brief history of American archaeology in Palestine by noting that it has had two streams. In addition to Biblical archaeology, there was a parallel secular stream, which included some of the most ambitious American work in the Middle East, though it has not always received the attention it deserves. It began in Palestine with Harvard University's excavations at Samaria in 1908–10, carried out by the brilliant archaeologist G. A. Reisner, who was years ahead of his time in method. There followed the large and lavish pre-World War II projects of Yale University at Jerash, ancient Gerasa, in Trans-Jordan (1928–34); of the University of Pennsylvania at Beth-Shan (1921–33); and especially of the Oriental Institute of the University of Chicago at the great site of Megiddo (1925–39). These excavations were exactly contemporary with those of Albright and the Biblical archaeologists in Palestine, though staffed and supported exclusively from secular sources. Yet the secular school, despite a more prestigious university base and more adequate financial backing, never really won the hearts of the American public the way the Biblical archaeology school of the same period did. That first generation in Palestinian archaeology simply could not replace itself, least of all after the War, when momentum had been lost.

By the 1950s, and into the 1960s, Biblical archaeology almost completely dominated American archaeology of Palestine. In Jordan, besides Wright's Harvard-Drew-McCormick excavations at Shechem (1956–68), there were excavations in the field carried out by James B. Pritchard, professor of religious thought at Pennsylvania, at el-Jib, Biblical Gibeon (1956–62); by Paul W. Lapp, for a consortium of Lutheran schools, at Taᶜanach, Rumeith, and elsewhere (1960–68); and by Joseph A. Callaway of Southern Baptist Theological Seminary at ᶜAi (1964–69). On a typical one of these excavations, funds would have come from Protestant seminaries, and the staff would have been made up almost exclusively of Biblical scholars, theologians, church historians, and the like. *All* these excavations were affiliated with the American Schools of Oriental Research in Jerusalem, direct successors of Albright's projects in the prewar years, in Biblical archaeology's golden age. The pattern seemed to be fixed; yet, as we shall now see, it changed rather abruptly in the late 1960s and 1970s. The new impetus came partly from American excavations in Israel, which did not really get under way until the mid-1960s. I will discuss those more thoroughly later on, after first addressing the current state of Syro-Palestinian archaeology.

Both internal and external developments have contributed to the strong tendency for the secular stream of Syro-Palestinian archaeology to overcome the stream of Biblical archaeology. An account of how this came about may begin with an assessment of the vulnerability of the Biblical archaeology school.

I have noted that by the 1950s there were sharp differences between the American and German schools, with Wright's distinctive American-style blend of Biblical archaeology and Biblical theology at the forefront. At issue here were not simply differing approaches to history writing, but fundamental divergences in theological presuppositions and methods. The specific issue was the "faith and history" theme so familiar in postwar Neo-Orthodoxy. The question was this: Is God's revelation of himself to be sought in the particular concrete events of *history* to which the Bible claims to bear witness, or rather in the community's *experience* of faith and redemption? Some critics suggested that Wright's eloquent evocation of "God's miraculous actions in history" was stirring as pulpit rhetoric, but somewhat disingenuous if it concealed the fact that Wright the modern historian and archaeologist did not really believe that those miracles had happened. Others pointed out theological weaknesses in Wright's conception of the possibility of historical confirmation of Biblical faith. Krister Stendahl, Wright's dean at Harvard, noted that "once we have accepted history as the fabric of biblical theology, we are thrown back to the same choice of faith which faced the first century. History does not answer such questions: it only poses them."[23] As I shall further argue below, even if archaeology could have demonstrated the historicity of Biblical events, that would not have confirmed the interpretation given to them by the Biblical writers, much less the modern church or synagogue. In fact, there is a school of thought that finds the very notion of "proving" the truth of the Bible inimical to Biblical faith. If we have proof, where is the need for belief?

Another difficulty which has plagued Biblical archaeology is its close alliance with a theological movement, the Protestant Biblical theology movement of the 1950s, in which Wright himself was a pivotal figure at the same time that he was a leading Palestinian archaeologist. The heated controversy over Biblical theology is beyond our purview here, but we may note that by the late 1960s this movement had exhausted itself, in large part over what seemed to be insoluble difficulties about how to write an adequate description of Israelite religion and move from that to normative theology. As Brevard Childs of Yale wrote in 1970 in *Biblical Theology in Crisis*, "the Biblical Theology Movement underwent a period of slow dissolution beginning in the late fifties. The breakdown resulted from pressure inside and outside that brought it to a virtual end as a major force in American theology in the early sixties."

It is significant that Wright himself moved steadily away from Biblical theology in his final years and toward his first love, archaeology. Whatever Wright's reasons, it was clear to others that the death of Biblical theology signaled the passing of a particular style of Biblical archaeology as well. In his last essays, written in the early 1970s, Wright makes no mention whatsoever of Biblical archaeology. He aligns himself rather with the "new archaeology" of that period, which we shall soon consider, and takes a much more modest position on what archaeology can contribute to faith. Above all, he commends those of his graduate students whom he sees as being in the vanguard of the revolutionary trends of the mid-1970s. With this development—the specialization of Wright's own students in archaeology, with his approval and not necessarily in combination with Biblical studies—an era was clearly ending. By the early 1970s I ventured to say in print what many had sensed: that Biblical archaeology as an academic discipline was dead. I did not kill it, as some have claimed. I'm flattered, but in truth I simply observed its passing and wrote its obituary.[24]

New historical considerations, as well as theological ones, accompanied these changes. In the 1930s Albright had coined the term "archaeological *revolution*" to describe the potential contribution of archaeology to Biblical studies. But in retrospect, the promised revolution never materialized. Albright's conception of Biblical archaeology was simply too ambitious a program to have been carried out. Research "from Gibraltar to the Indus valley, from 10,000 B.C. almost to the present" would have taxed the range even of an Albright—and he has no successors. "Biblical archaeology" came to mean the *whole* of ancient Near Eastern studies, and nobody could do it all. The inevitable specialization that followed had the effect of rendering the grand design not so much untenable as simply unattainable, and therefore irrelevant. History could not be written on so broad a canvas, at least by a single school, much less an individual.

A second difficulty with Biblical archaeology as a putative historical discipline was that it lacked a raison d'être of its own, that is, as either archaeology or history. It was, as we have seen, a reactionary movement in Biblical studies. It took its agenda from certain problems then current in Biblical history and interpretation. But it had no independent method or objectives, and thus no reason for continuing to exist after those controversies had either been resolved or faded away. The passing of biblical theology left Biblical archaeology stranded, without an adequate rationale for existing.

A third weakness was its parochialism. Its practitioners were almost exclusively Protestant, post-Liberal, Old Testament scholars. Furthermore, in the form it had taken by the 1950s it was a peculiarly American phenomenon; it had no real counterparts in Europe or the Middle East, where archaeology had been and remained a largely secular enterprise. Could an approach as narrow as the American commend itself as a universal option for the field? Within Syro-Palestinian archaeology, Biblical archaeology represented a minority opinion, which made it seem even less viable than it had first appeared. It became obvious to many that there could and should be other approaches.

But the most serious objection to Biblical archaeology arose from its failure to solve the basic historical problems to which it had set itself under Albright's aegis. These were, of course, the questions of the historicity of the Patriarchal, Mosaic, and Conquest eras—Israel's most remote and perplexing historical epochs, but also those thought most amenable to archaeological investigation (see chapter 2).

Again, we cannot trace in detail the efforts of Biblical archaeology over the past sixty years to confirm the historicity of personalities and events of these eras. The most recent survey of the archaeological background of the Patriarchal period is one that I was recently asked to do for a basic handbook of Israelite and Judean history. I set out thinking that perhaps it was possible, after all, to defend Albright's attempt to locate the Patriarchs within a particular archaeological-historical phase in Palestine (i.e., the Middle Bronze I or perhaps II period). After an exhaustive survey of the evidence and of recent scholarly opinion, however, I had to conclude that we are farther than ever from a solution to this problem. On the one hand, the narratives of Genesis are a composite of many layers of oral and written tradition, from many different time periods and social circumstances. It is thus impossible to isolate a kernel of truth and assign that to one specific period on the basis of historical "fit." On the other hand, while archaeology has been able to document in general the pastoral nomadic lifestyle depicted in Genesis throughout the second millennium B.C. (and other periods), it has not brought to light any direct evidence to substantiate the story that an Abraham lived, that he migrated from Mesopotamia to Canaan, or that there was a Joseph who found his way to Egypt and rose to power there. The point is not that archaeology has disproved the historicity of the Patriarchs, but simply that it has not gotten beyond the literary tradition that we had all along in the Hebrew Bible. The tradition is made up of legends that still may be regarded as containing moral truths, but until now they have been of uncertain historical provenance. [25]

On Albright's favorite theme, "Moses and monotheism," the silence of archaeology is even more profound. Absolutely no trace of Moses, or indeed of an Israelite presence in Egypt, has ever turned up. Of the exodus and the wandering in the wilderness—events so crucial in the Biblical recitation of the "mighty acts of God"—we have no evidence whatsoever; nor are we likely to have any, since slaves, serfs, and nomads leave few traces in the archaeological record. Recent Israeli excavations at Kadesh-barnea, the Sinai oasis where the Israelites are said to have encamped for forty years, have revealed an extensive settlement, but not so much as a potsherd earlier than the tenth century B.C. Finally, we must confess that the origins of Israelite monotheism, while no doubt much earlier than some Biblical critics had first thought, are as much a mystery as ever. And archaeology, by its very nature, cannot be expected to enlighten us much on this question, since it deals largely with material culture remains, or at best with patterns of behavior, not with ideology per se.

Finally, the Israelite settlement in Palestine, to which I shall devote my second chapter, has received intense scholarly attention in the last two generations. Dozens of late Canaanite and early Israelite settlements have been excavated, and hundreds more have been surveyed in surface exploration. Yet here again the evidence is largely negative. In particular, the "conquest model" of Albright and Wright, derived principally from the book of Joshua, has been largely discredited. That Israel did emerge in Canaan in the early Iron Age is beyond doubt. But archaeology has not shown that the process of settlement followed a series of destructions, miraculous or otherwise.

I cannot end this critique of Biblical archaeology without noting the recent, widespread reaction against Albright and his school. This was apparent in Europe by the 1950s, and it is now seen in much of the literature in Biblical studies in America, beginning in the 1970s. The most striking instance was seen, I think, only a few months ago, at a symposium actually honoring Albright. A principal speaker was David Noel Freedman, one of the staunchest members and most eloquent defenders of the Albright school, who only a few years ago was promoting the cuneiform texts found recently by Italian excavators at Ebla, near Aleppo in Syria, as proof of the historicity of the Patriarchs. Freedman made the following remarks, which I will quote at some length, since his comments are candid and very revealing:

> The combination of the Bible and archaeology is somewhat artificial; the two have not really matched up very well. The Biblical scholar deals with one kind of material and the archaeologist with another. On rare but important occasions, there is significant contact, and both disciplines gain from the exchange of data and ideas. Often, however, there is no point of contact and nothing significant happens. On the whole, I believe that results of the interchange between archaeology and the Bible have been somewhat disappointing, though perhaps that was to be expected. Palestinian archaeology

has had modest success in turning up monumental remains and inscriptional materials, but nothing like the quantity discovered in Mesopotamia and Egypt. Unwritten materials are extensive in Palestine, to be sure, but not always easy to interpret, and the Biblical connections remain elusive while confirmations are few and far between.

Albright's great plan and expectation to set the Bible firmly on the foundation of archaeology buttressed by verifiable data seems to have foundered or at least floundered. After all the digging, done and being done and yet to be done, how much has been accomplished? The fierce debates and arguments about the relevance of archaeology to the Bible and vice versa indicate that many issues remain unresolved. Can anyone say anything with confidence about the patriarchs or the patriarchal age? The fact that skeptical voices now dominate the scene indicates that the Albrightian synthesis has become unglued and we are further from a solution than we ever were. Archaeology has not proved decisive or even greatly helpful in answering the questions most often asked and has failed to prove the historicity of Biblical persons and events, especially in the early periods.[26]

Note Freedman's frank admission of exactly what I have been saying about the failure of the older style Biblical archaeology. But he is too negative. He complains, first of all, that archaeology was not capable of "answering the questions most often asked" by Biblical scholars, and secondly that archaeology did not "prove the historicity of Biblical persons and events." My response is that the wrong questions were being asked. Further, it should never have been supposed that the purpose of archaeology was to "prove" the Bible in any sense. It was not archaeology that failed, but rather a generation of Biblical scholars who misunderstood and misapplied this valuable tool—largely because most never developed beyond amateur status. Worse still, some Biblical scholars actively opposed the growth of Palestinian archaeology as an independent, professional discipline, and thus found themselves left behind. It is my purpose in this work to outline a new approach to Biblical archaeology, one that I am confident will break through the impasse that Freedman describes.

There were not only internal weaknesses in Biblical archaeology, but also several unexpected developments outside the field that brought change. At the very time when American Biblical archaeology found itself combating collapse from within, there were powerful external forces at work that would soon revive the old secular stream of Syro-Palestinian archaeology as formidable competition. The five chief factors in this new development of the late 1960s and 1970s were as follows.[27] (Perhaps I may be forgiven for relating many of these trends to our excavations at Gezer from 1964 through 1973, for this project became a bellwether of the "new archaeology.")

First, large-scale American excavations began in Israel in the early 1960s, supplementing those already under way in Jordan. The result was that the American school, still dominated by the objectives and methods of Biblical archaeology, now came into increasing contact and competition with other foreign and national schools in the Middle East, including not only British, French, and other European schools, but also the local schools, especially the large, vigorous, and well-supported "Israeli school." All had differing approaches, and none did American-style Biblical archaeology—not even the Israelis, who did employ the Bible in archaeology, but more as a document of national history than as theological or confessional literature. The Israeli school, despite tracing its roots back to Albright, was unabashedly secular—so much so that when Ernest Wright and his students began working in Israel at Gezer in 1964 the Israelis were baffled by archaeologists who were clergymen. Could anyone even imagine an Israeli rabbi-archaeologist? And later, in the 1970s, Americans working in the Arab countries ran into stiff opposition from Jordanian and Syrian archaeologists, who quite understandably wanted little to do with the Bible, and nothing whatsoever to do with the question of Israelite origins. Thus there appeared options other than traditional American-style Biblical archaeology.

The second factor, the advent of student volunteerism, was less predictable. Largely because of a shortage of skilled laborers, like the well-known Arab "technical men" in Jordan, we began at Gezer by organizing the entire dig as a summer field school and carrying out all the work in the trench with unpaid student labor, mostly American. This idea caught on and rapidly transformed the typical American dig in Israel from an employer-employee experience into an outdoor classroom learning experience—with the staff surprisingly learning as much as it taught. The irreverent, persistent questions of bright young people with no commitment to our field, most of them secularists, forced our senior staff—all trained as Biblical scholars—to rethink their own motives and methods. We now had to defend ourselves *as archaeologists*, or not at all. Little did we realize when we first took on the training of students in the field that our own conception of what we were doing would change so radically.

The third factor was the continued commitment to methodological innovation. This had been typical of previous American fieldwork in Jordan and Israel, but heretofore the emphasis had been primarily on learning how to dig a complex mound-site well—that is, stratigraphy—and secondarily on perfecting ceramic typology, or pottery sequence-dating. We called this "methodology," but it was really more practical technique: a distinctly American, pragmatic approach. Now, however, the next logical step moved us closer to a real consideration of basic archaeological theory, as well as to newer analytical methods in research. Having learned how to separate earth layers cleanly and how to sample and record all the various materials they contained, what were we to make of the carefully accumulated raw data? A modern dig was now capable of producing a mass of well-dated remains, including not only the architecture, pottery, and small finds formerly saved, but sedimentary deposits of all kinds, animal and human bones, seed samples, and countless new categories of evidence. Thus out of necessity, as early as 1966, we began to adopt at Gezer the *multidisciplinary* approach that had already come into vogue with the new archaeology in America. Very shortly one saw, working alongside Biblical archaeologists, staff members who were geologists, geomorphologists, climatologists, economic geographers, paleobotanists and paleozoologists, physical and cultural anthropologists, historians of technology, and, finally, computer programers to help record, process, and analyze this mass of data. More than any other single factor in the 1970s, the new multidisciplinary approach—especially the ecological thrust that sought to study ancient sites in their total setting, natural, cultural, and historical—made Biblical archaeology obsolete. The old questions were too narrow; not only did they finally prove uninteresting, but the preoccupation with political history had meant that more evidence was discarded than collected. No longer would that be conscionable; Biblical history was important, but so were many other research aims.

The fourth trend that brought change was the need to find secular sources of funding, as the cost of careful fieldwork, large multidisciplinary staffs, and elaborate field schools mounted astronomically. By the early 1970s, the annual budget of a typical large American excavation in Israel or Jordan exceeded a hundred thousand dollars—far beyond the resources of the consortium of seminaries and small church colleges that had sponsored digs in the 1950s and 1960s. We had to turn to new sources, principally federal funds disbursed at first through the Smithsonian Institution, and later through the National Endowment for the Humanities. When applying to such sources, simply "digging up Biblical history" was not an adequate rationale; we had to learn to do "problem-solving" archaeology, with problems of interest to others, to write (and carry out) sophisticated research designs that could compete in the rigorous peer review process of American academic archaeology and anthropology. Secular funding certainly helped to foster a secular approach.

The final factor in the transformation of Biblical archaeology only began to have an impact in the late 1970s and has yet to materialize fully. This was the belated adaptation of aspects of what was called the "new archaeology" in America, which had been around since the 1960s. This revolutionary movement is far too complex, and still too controversial, to be described here. We should note, however, that the major innovations in new archaeology by the more avant-garde Syro-Palestinian specialists in the 1970s were all based on assumptions borrowed—often naïvely or even unconsciously—from American anthropology and archaeology. The changes were seen most obviously in: the multidisciplinary orientation; the broader consideration of environmental factors ("ecology"); the increased recognition of the value of ethnographic parallels ("ethnoarchaeology"); the employment of general systems theory (a "holistic" or systemic theory of culture); the logic of "explicitly scientific" method, with its hypothesis testing; and the adoption of the "behavioral-processualist" model (from one school of cultural anthropology). These are precisely the fundamental tenets of the new archaeology of the 1960s in America. Only the overriding evolutionary framework was missing, and that had been more or less presumed in Near Eastern archaeology from the beginning.

In summary, the new archaeology was much less narrowly historical in orientation, more allied with anthropology and increasingly with the other social and natural sciences. This approach to archaeology, pioneered largely on small, single-period New World sites, could not (and should not) be simply transplanted to Middle Eastern sites, with their complex depositional nature and long history in written records. But the new archaeology has already taught us to ask new and vastly more far-reaching questions of our data. Furthermore, it has forced us to be self-critical, especially in making explicit our research aims and methods—one of its greatest benefits. Finally, the adoption of research aims and methods related to new questions has brought former Biblical archaeologists—and especially the younger generation and our current graduate students—further into the mainstream of American archaeology as pursued in secular universities and elsewhere in academe. Even though it is not yet clear where this new secular discipline is going or where it will find support, American Palestinian archaeology has at last come out of the cloister, into the academy, and even the marketplace.

The cumulative effect of the trends of the 1970s sketched above was to bring about the separation of Biblical archaeology into two disciplines: Biblical studies, and archaeology. For the latter discipline most of us in the field advocate the term "Syro-Palestinian archaeology"—Albright's original name, and the one preferred all along by the secular branch of archaeology in America and elsewhere. This field has now begun to develop rapidly as an independent, highly specialized, professional academic discipline. It is no longer conceived as an amateur pursuit, much less as simply a branch of Biblical studies, but rather as a branch of Near Eastern archaeology, i.e., that subfield that deals with the specific geographical-cultural entity known since classical times as Syria-Palestine, including the Biblical lands and peoples but by no means confined to these.

It was said by the Albright-Wright school that "archaeology is the handmaiden of history." But now archaeology is no longer a *sub*-discipline of anything. It is itself a discipline, multidisciplinary in its relationship to other fields of inquiry (including Biblical studies), but with its own appropriate and independent rationale, objectives, and methods. Hereafter "Biblical archaeology" would not so much denote an academic discipline—certainly not a surrogate for the broader field now defined more properly as Syro-Palestinian archaeology—but rather a *dialogue between two disciplines*. As we shall see, although it was threatening to many and accompanied by the usual growing pains, the coming of age of Syro-Palestinian archaeology was not only inevitable but actually beneficial.[28]

On the Proper Relation of Syro-Palestinian Archaeology to Biblical Studies

Since I have been the most vocal advocate of the separation of Syro-Palestinian archaeology from Biblical studies, I must now show how a new and more productive relationship between these two disciplines may be conceived.

The model I propose is that of a new dialogue between two equal partners, having similar concerns but each with its own approach and individual contribution to make. Since the older conception tended to view archaeology as one aspect of Biblical studies, most discussions of Biblical archaeology were monologues, written by and for Biblical scholars. At best, the participants were merely amateur archaeologists, who had not themselves excavated the evidence they adduced, could not control it in a critical or comparative manner, and in fact knew very little of real archaeological method. (This "applied archaeology" was what Wright had lauded as "armchair archaeology," but by today's standards most of it was incompetent.) At worst, in Biblical archaeology theological presuppositions—perhaps subconscious, but obvious to any outside observer—determined the outcome of the inquiry. The result, as we have seen, was that most attempts to relate archaeology to Biblical history were controversial and finally inconclusive. And many, unfortunately, discredited the whole enterprise.

A dialogue, by definition, can proceed only from the articulation of differing and independent points of view. The obvious solution to the frustration produced by recent treatments of Biblical archaeology requires that we distinguish two fundamental disciplines, define each in terms of its autonomous objectives and methods, and allow each to develop according to its own canons. This is not to isolate archaeology from Biblical studies, as some fear, but rather to clear the way for a true dialogue, one that will respect the integrity of both disciplines and profit from the specialized knowledge of each. The question is not whether Syro-Palestinian archaeology can be related to Biblical studies (it can and must be), but how. The dialogue I have envisioned between two separate disciplines was actually called for many years before, when the excesses of Biblical archaeology were already apparent to some Biblical scholars. In his 1968 presidential address to the Society of Biblical Literature, Morton Smith very sensibly observed that "for a correct history of the Israelites we must have the archaeological facts determined quite objectively and independently by competent archaeologists, and the biblical facts likewise determined by competent philologians, and then we can begin to compare them."[29] But twenty years ago Smith was a voice crying in the wilderness.

The remaining chapters in this book will explore three specific areas to show just how this dialogue, only now beginning, may proceed. Here I shall only offer a general outline of the appropriate relation between our two disciplines. Since I speak as a practicing archaeologist, I shall confine myself largely to that discipline, assuming that it can contribute to Biblical studies, but defining its role by showing both its possibilities and its limitations. The positive contributions of archaeology are all historical, not theological.

First, archaeology has restored the Bible to its original setting by recovering the forgotten peoples, places, and cultures of the Ancient Near East—the long-lost world in which Israel originated and her life and literature took form and meaning. The Bible is no longer an isolated relic from antiquity, without provenance and thus without credibility. Archaeology may not have proven the specific historical existence of certain Biblical personalities such as Abraham or Moses, but it has for all time demolished the notion that the Bible is pure mythology. The Bible is about real, flesh-and-blood people, in a particular time and place, whose actual historical experience led them irrevocably to a vision of the human condition and promise that transcended anything yet conceived in antiquity.

Beyond illustrating the Biblical world generally, however, archaeology has made more specific contributions. The cumulative discoveries of archaeology over the past century have brought back to life Israel's neighboring ancient Near Eastern cultures. This has given us a context in which we can study Israel comparatively, and thereby appreciate more fully both her similarities to other peoples and her distinctive differences. More recently, multidisciplinary archaeology has begun to recover not just isolated events in ancient Israel, but the larger context in which they took place. We now can reconstruct Israel's environmental setting—topography, climate, land and water resources, subsistence systems, exchange networks, settlement patterns, demography, and the like. Thus, at last, archaeology begins to have the potential to deal with "the ecology of socio-economic change." These environmental factors in the shaping of culture we may call "ecofacts," largely ignored until recently, but just as important as artifacts or textual facts. Rather than focusing simply on the impact of the actions of great kings and priests, or the role of religious ideology, looking at sites in their natural and historical setting can lead us to an understanding of the total dynamics of cultural change. We can now see Israel in another of its aspects, as a secular society. For us moderns to appreciate Israel's uniqueness and her evolution as a society, this secular approach is absolutely essential. But it is not made possible by the information that the Bible itself supplies, only by the external evidence brought to light by archaeology.

Second, even in the narrower, more traditional context of comment on Biblical texts, archaeology still provides an invaluable service. Countless hitherto enigmatic passages have been clarified by the discovery of either parallel non-Biblical texts, or artifacts that actually illustrate the text for the first time. The translation of the term *pîm* in I Samuel 13:19–21 was pure guesswork until archaeologists brought to light small stone balance weights inscribed in Paleo-Hebrew with the word *pîm*, which we now know designates a silver shekel fraction of ca. 7.8 grams. The discovery of dozens of fourteenth-century B.C. mythological texts from Ugarit, on the coast of Syria, from 1929 onward has revolutionized translation and understanding of the Book of Psalms, as well as the early Hebrew poetry of the Pentateuch. At Ugarit we are suddenly transported back into the conceptual world of Canaanite culture from which ancient Israel emerged, and we can glimpse Israel's poetic literature from a viewpoint at least six centuries closer to its source. We can thus strip away layers of accretions to the Biblical text, seeing how later copyists and commentators perpetuated mistaken or misleading interpretations, or, in some cases, deliberate alterations to the text. Indeed, one of archaeology's most significant contributions to Biblical studies in the twentieth century has been in the field of textual and form criticism.

Even where certain Biblical passages are correctly understood, they may remain unappreciated as historical sources simply because they are unconfirmed. A single case would be the passage in I Kings 9:15–17, describing Solomon's takeover of Gezer after an Egyptian destruction and his refortification of the site, along with Jerusalem, Hazor, and Megiddo. This detail, scarcely of interest to the Biblical chronicler, passed almost unnoticed until modern archaeologists uncovered similar Solomonic city gates and walls at Hazor and Megiddo, then an Egyptian destruction and nearly identical city walls and gate at Gezer.[30] Here we have confirmation of a neglected, rather laconic footnote to Biblical history, the more dramatic because it was totally unexpected: no one had set out to prove the historicity of this text. How many more such surprises await us as archaeology progresses? My point is that even if archaeology cannot confirm the ultimate religious meaning of the Bible overall, it can nevertheless clarify the historical circumstances of numerous individual texts and the events they describe.

Third, archaeology cannot comment on all or even the majority of the Biblical texts, but it can supply missing elements of the story, and in some cases even an alternate version. It can add matters in which the Biblical writers were simply not interested, or events of which they may have been unaware. This supplementary or corrective (rather than corroborative) aspect of archaeology is often neglected, but in reality it is one of its most valuable features for amplifying and illuminating the Biblical text. An example of supplementary evidence is seen in the fall of Lachish to Sennacherib in 701 B.C.—an event of devasting importance to Judah, but not even alluded to in the one reference in II Kings 18:14, which simply states that the Assyrian king was "at Lachish" during a Judean campaign. Archaeology has uncovered, however, two extra-Biblical sources that dramatically confirm a severe destruction of Lachish at this time: eyewitness pictorial representations in the famous Lachish reliefs, actually mentioning Lachish, found in the palace of the Assyrian kings at Nimrud; and the vivid evidence of the destruction of Level III found by both the British and the current Israeli excavations at the site itself— some of the most eloquent and moving remains of a destruction ever found. Why do the Biblical writers make no mention of this event? It may, of course be partly due to the fact that for them the real story concerned the miraculous lifting of the siege of Jerusalem. The silence may also be due to an understandable reluctance to give coverage to a shameful defeat. Yet without the contribution of archaeology, we would know nothing whatsoever of the fall of Lachish.[31] An example of corrective evidence is seen in the rich material remains of the local cults, some semi-pagan, that archaeology has uncovered in ancient Israel—this in spite of the picture the Biblical writers usually give us of a centralized Yahwistic cult in Jerusalem. (I shall devote a later chapter to this topic.)

Finally, although archaeology cannot necessarily illuminate ancient theology, much less create modern belief, it can and does reveal material culture—the common everyday life of the average Israelite or Judean, the stuff of real life. This is not to down-play the role of ideology, or the otherworldly aspects of Biblical religion. It is simply to affirm the astute observation of Norman Gottwald in his magnum opus, *The Tribes of Yahweh*: "Only as the full *materiality* of ancient Israel is more securely grasped will we be able to make proper sense of its *spirituality*."[32] The Bible's preoccupation with ideas is complemented perfectly by archaeology's capability of bringing to light realia.

To sum up: archaeology, insofar as it is a historical discipline, is uniquely equipped to help answer such questions in Biblical studies as these: What likely took place? When did it occur? Who were the principal participants? How did it happen? But here archaeology reaches the limits of its inquiry. It cannot, and is not intended to, answer the question, Why?—certainly not in terms of ultimate or divine causes. Such questions call for judgments of faith, whose validity archaeology seeks neither to prove nor to disprove.

I have always found it helpful to separate two tasks facing me as a scholar and as an individual. First is the descriptive-historical task, the business of the historian, who must be as objective as possible in finding out what happened and asking, "What *did* it mean?" Then there is the normative-theological task, part of the process of reaching a value judgment when asking, "What *does* it mean?" One person can function at both levels, but not simultaneously. Questions of faith, while paramount to me, are not necessarily related to my historical research, nor are my conclusions authoritative for anyone else. It is incumbent upon me to suspend judgment on questions of faith while I, as archaeologist and scholar, pursue the historical quest for which I have been professionally prepared.

2

THE ISRAELITE
SETTLEMENT
IN
CANAAN

New Archaeological Models

THERE are no more crucial problems in the study of ancient Israelite history and religion than those that pertain to the settlement in Canaan. This is the earliest, most formative horizon that we can recover historically, the one in which the distinctive entity known as "Israel" arose, two centuries before the formation of the Israelite state. At the same time, the theological inferences drawn later from events of this era constitute the very heart of Israel's radically historical faith. Here the theme of the Promised Land is the very essence of God's covenant with the Patriarchs, reaffirmed to Moses, fulfilled in Joshua. Its culmination is seen in the deliverance of a nameless band of slaves from Egypt, their crossing of the Red Sea and wandering in the wilderness, and finally their miraculous conquest of the land of Canaan with its apportionment among the twelve tribes. These events, however we understand them, were for ancient Israel the historical confirmation of her election as the chosen people of Yahweh, the very foundation of her existence. The central proclamation of the Hebrew Bible is the claim that God revealed himself uniquely in the Exodus and Conquest; all else is commentary.[1] The brief historical credo that scholars have isolated in Deuteronomy 6:20–25 summarizes Israel's primitive faith.

> When your son asks you in time to come, "What is the meaning of the testimonies and the statutes and the ordinances which the Lord our God has commanded you?" then you shall say to your son, "We were Pharaoh's slaves in Egypt; and the Lord brought us out of Egypt with a mighty hand; and the Lord showed signs and wonders, great and grievous, against Egypt and against Pharaoh and all his household, before our eyes; and he brought us out from there, that he might bring us in and give us the land which he swore to give to our fathers. And the Lord commanded us to do all these statutes, to fear the Lord our God, for our good always, that he might preserve us alive, as at this day. And it will be righteousness for us, if we are careful to do all these commandments before the Lord our God, as he has commanded us." (RSV)

But can archaeology offer any confirmation of that claim, or even, for that matter, bring us any closer to a description of the actual process of Israel's emergence in Canaan? This pivotal problem in early Israelite history will provide an ideal test case for the newer archaeological approach outlined in chapter 1. Let us turn, then, to the textual, the artifactual, and the environmental data, in an attempt to see how these sources of evidence interact to shed new light on the period of the settlement around 1200 B.C.

The Nature of the Evidence:
Older Reconstructions (ca. 1930–1960)

The first category of evidence comes from the Biblical texts themselves. The material that covers events from the last phases of the wandering in the wilderness through the conquest and settlement of Canaan is contained exclusively in Numbers 13–31, the book of Joshua, and the first chapter of Judges. These primary sources can be divided conveniently into two differing and in many ways contradictory versions of what took place.

The Numbers-Joshua version begins with Numbers 13, which has the Israelite tribes poised at the oasis of Kadesh-barnea on the border of the Sinai and Negev deserts. Numbers then continues with the well-known account of the sending out of the spies; the disenchantment of the people with Moses' and Aaron's leadership; the crossing of the northern Negev and the first victories over the Canaanites at Arad and Hormah; the encounters with the Amorites and Midianites, especially with the Moabites at Heshbon and elsewhere, then later to the north in Ammon and Bashan; the census in Moab, anticipating the crossing of the Jordan (hence the "numbers"); and the final ritual preparations for holy war in the camp opposite Jericho in the Jordan Valley. Here Numbers ends.

In the present arrangement of books in the Hebrew Bible, Deuteronomy follows Numbers, but modern scholarship has shown that this is largely a later block of material, a lengthy sermon put into the mouth of Moses, actually dating from the seventh century B.C. and placed here by the Deuteronomic editors of the Pentateuch. The thread of our story really resumes with the final chapter of Deuteronomy, which recounts the death of Moses in Trans-Jordan. There follows immediately the book of Joshua, which extols the deeds of Moses' successor in conquering the Canaanites west of the Jordan. According to this version, the conquest was a planned, rapid, and complete rout of the Canaanites, an effort of all twelve tribes (or "all Israel") acting in concert under Joshua, with Israel emerging as the undisputed military master of the land both west and east of the Jordan.

The book of Joshua is divided into three campaigns. First there is a central campaign beginning with the crossing of the Jordan and the fall of Jericho, the capture of ʿAi and Gibeon, and the thrust up into the hills around Jerusalem (Joshua 1–10:29). Then there is a southern campaign in which it is claimed that the Israelites took such cities as Makkedah, Libnah, Lachish, Eglon, Hebron, and Debir (10:28–43). Finally, there is a lightning raid to the north, in which the principal victory was the fall of the great city-state of Hazor, "the head of all those kingdoms" (11–13:7). The remainder of Joshua (13:8–19:51) is taken up with the apportionment of the former land of Canaan among the twelve tribes of Israel. The book closes with Joshua's farewell address to a triumphant Israel and his death.

The second version of the so-called conquest of Canaan, contained in the book of Judges, is strikingly different. It knows nothing of successful military campaigns under Joshua and indeed begins its story in the very first verse with the death of Joshua. The remainder of chapter 1 retells some of the individual, isolated conquests of the book of Joshua, such as the capture of Jerusalem, Hebron, and Debir. But for the most part the account stresses the inability of the Israelites to take effective possession of the land. Again and again, sites not captured are listed (thirty in all), and the writers repeatedly invoke a fixed formula to state that "the Canaanites were not driven out, and they dwell in ———— to this day." Several verses of chapter 1 note that Israelites and Canaanites continued to dwell side by side. Furthermore, the entire remainder of the book of Judges is the story of a series of crises provoked when the Canaanites threatened to overwhelm the Israelites dispersed among them. These emergencies were met only as the tribes rallied to charismatic leaders raised up by Yahweh to lead the tribal confederation in holy war—figures such as Deborah, Gideon, Samson, and others. These *shôphētim*, or "Judges," were really successive militia leaders, who led occasional successful forays against the entrenched Canaanites, but never won decisive battles, and soon faded into the background again. Several sites are listed as having been taken more than once, others not at all. And it is clear that the entire span of the twelve judges covers the early twelfth to the late tenth centuries B.C.—nearly two hundred years of unremitting struggle. As the book of Judges observes of the end of this period of tribal disunity and humiliation, "in those days there was no king in Israel, and every man did what was right in his own eyes." The book of Judges, with its account of gradual Israelite infiltration and assimilation in Canaan, is diametrically opposed to the story of Joshua, which is one of overwhelming military victories. There seems to be no way in which these two opposing versions of what happened can be reconciled. Which (if either) is true? And which does archaeology support?

Before attempting to answer the historical question, let us look briefly at the assessment of the Biblical traditions by literary and form critics. It is the general consensus of scholarly opinion that both Numbers and Joshua-Judges 1 belong to a larger work known as the Hexateuch (i.e., the Pentateuch, plus Joshua-Judges 1). Also regarded as the Deuteronomic History, this is a composite work, based on two older epic sources we call J and E, dating from the ninth and tenth centuries B.C., combined and edited by an archaizing reform school of Mosaic writers in the late seventh century B.C. The older theme of "peaceful infiltration," from the Judges material, certainly the more realistic of the two, is still preserved here; but the Deuteronomists have overlain it with a more artificial and indeed propagandistic account accentuating the "conquest" and "all Israel" themes, and glorifying Moses' successor Joshua.[2]

Until about a hundred years ago, we possessed not so much as a single extra-Biblical text concerning the Exodus and conquest; the Hebrew Bible was our sole literary and historical witness, and thus suspect in the eyes of many. Today, however, we have a relative abundance of pertinent textual data, nearly all of it from Egypt.

First, there are several Egyptian New Kingdom topographical texts that describe general conditions and even specify various ethnic groups in Palestine in the immediate preceding period, the Late Bronze Age (ca. the thirteenth and fourteenth centuries B.C.). Foremost among these are the various Papyri Anastasi. But there are also similar hieroglyphic references on major monuments in Egypt.[3]

Even more important are the famous Amarna Letters, some three-hundred-fifty cuneiform tablets found in 1878 by an Egyptian peasant woman. They came from the ruins of the palace at el-Amarna, which belonged to Akhnaten, Nefertiti's husband, the famous "heretic king" who introduced the worship of the Aten/sun-disc as the sole deity. These fourteenth-century B.C. tablets are written in Akkadian, an east Semitic language of Mesopotamia that had become the language of international diplomatic correspondence by the Late Bronze Age. Although found in Egypt, these letters are from various kings and petty princes in Syria-Palestine, addressed to the Pharaoh and deposited in his palace archives at el-Amarna, where they lay neglected (and unanswered). Since Palestine was then part of the Egyptian New Kingdom empire in Asia, the Amarna Letters are mostly appeals to the Egyptian overlord for military id and economic assistance. But in the course of reporting to the Pharaon, the Syro-Palestinian rulers convey detailed, intimate, often fascinating information about political, social, and economic conditions in Canaan some two centuries before the earliest appearance of the Israelites. The Amarna Letters are thus a gold mine for the Biblical historian, and numerous twentieth-century scholars have attempted to use them to reconstruct the background of the Israelite settlement in Canaan, as we shall see when we come to evaluate these letters in the light of the archaeological evidence. In particular, scholars have long been fascinated by a socio-economic class or group which appears in the Amarna Letters as a lawless, rebellious element. They are called the ʿApiru. Could these possibly be the ancestors of the later Israelites, the Proto-Hebrews?[4]

Still more striking is the well-known Victory Stela of Pharaoh Merneptah (ca. 1212–02 B.C.), of the XIX Dynasty. This monument, dating to the pharaoh's fifth year—ca. 1207 B.C.—contains the earliest known actual reference to "Israel" outside the Bible. The pertinent section reads:

> The Princes are prostrate, saying "Peace!"
> Not one raises his head among the Nine Bows.
> Desolate is Tehenu; Hatti is pacified;
> Plundered is Canaan with every evil;
> Carried off is Ashkelon; seized upon is Gezer;
> Yanoam is made as that which does not exist;
> Israel is laid waste, his seed is not.[5]

This text is especially significant because it shows beyond doubt that by about 1210 B.C. at the latest a group of people known collectively as Israel was sufficiently established in Canaan that they were considered a possible threat to Egyptian hegemony. The date of the Merneptah reference remains our best fixed point of reference for the emergence of Israel.

A final Egyptian text, slightly later, comes from the walls of the temple at Medinet Habu, near Luxor. It recounts in both inscriptions and pictorial representations the great battle of ca. 1175 B.C., when Ramses III, in his eighth year, repelled an invasion of "Sea Peoples" (immigrants to the eastern Mediterranean coast) by land and sea. Among these groups specific mention is made of the Philistines, who appear in the Bible as Israel's contemporaries and competitors in the struggle to wrest early Iron Age Palestine from the Canaanites.[6]

The cumulative evidence of the above and other texts brought to light by archaeology has been not only to place the Israelite settlement in Palestine for the first time on firmer historical ground, but also to provide a fixed date coinciding with an archaeological phase, i.e., the transition from the Late Bronze to the Iron Age, ca. 1200 B.C.

Let us now turn, however, to the more strictly artifactual data recovered from the archaeological record, in order to understand the process. Archaeology, apart from producing textual finds, did not begin to provide a historical basis for the Israelite settlement in Canaan until the 1930s. As explained in the first chapter, it was Albright and his disciples who undertook the investigation as a principal item on the agenda of Biblical archaeology, because of the pivotal importance of the conquest-settlement for early Israelite history, and indeed for Israelite religion.

The first historical problem to be faced was that of determining the date of the Exodus and Conquest. Until the 1940s or later, the Exodus was placed in the mid-fifteenth century—at 1447 B.C., to be precise. This date was based primarily on one system of correlating the various Biblical chronologies, despite their many contradictions; and secondarily on the connection, made since Josephus's time, of the "descent of Joseph into Egypt" with the rise of the Semitic rulers known as the "Hyksos" in the XV Dynasty, ca. 1650–1550 B.C.

One still occasionally sees the fifteenth century B.C. date of the Exodus defended by Fundamentalists, but other scholars have long since given it up. The Merneptah stela discussed above suggested a later date, as did the definitive dating of the contemporaries of the Israelites, the Philistines, to the early twelfth century B.C. Also, the references to the cities of "Pithom and Ramses" in the Biblical narratives describing the camp of the Israelites in the Delta (Exodus 1:11) can be correlated only with the Egyptian occupation of this area in the XIX Dynasty under Ramses II, ca. 1279–13 B.C., who must then have been the notorious pharaoh of the exodus from Egypt. But the decisive factor was the mounting evidence in the 1930s that only one stratigraphic and cultural break in the excavated sites of the mid- to late second millennium B.C. in Western Palestine could possibly provide a setting for major ethnic movements: the transition from the Late Bronze to the Iron Age. This break was dated to ca. 1200 B.C. not only by the ceramic dating progressively refined by Albright and others, but also by Egyptian dating evidence found in destruction layers that were then first coming to light, such as that at Lachish. In Eastern Palestine, meanwhile, Nelson Glueck's explorations in the 1930s and 1940s demonstrated that there was no appreciable Late Bronze occupation in southern Trans-Jordan, thus no possible historical-archaeological context for the Israelite campaigns there, until the early Iron Age, ca. 1200 B.C. or shortly thereafter. In summary, one of the great success stories of modern archaeology is the correlation of the historical background of the Israelite settlement with a precise archaeological phase in Palestine, despite the fact that the Biblical records alone gave us little hope of such precision.[7]

But what of the actual process of the settlement? The second thrust of Palestinian archaeology in its formative years in the 1930s was to test a model for understanding the Israelite settlement against the evidence accumulating from the excavated mounds. Albright's model was that of the "conquest theory" of the book of Joshua, so he and his followers concentrated on Late Bronze Age/Iron I destruction layers—almost to the exclusion of other models or evidence contrary to their model.

The essentials of Albright's argument were all worked out in the 1930s on the basis of excavations being done at that time, and they were modified only slightly in subsequent years. In his own excavation from 1926 to 1932 at Tell Beit Mirsim, which Albright identified as Biblical Debir, the Late Bronze Age city was found to have been destroyed about 1200 B.C. Above the destruction level (Stratum C$_2$) there was a brief squatter occupation of the early twelfth century B.C., characterized principally by pits (Stratum B$_3$), then a later Iron I established settlement with Philistine bichrome pottery (Stratum B$_2$). The sequence at Tell Beit Mirsim was proof for Albright that Debir had been destroyed by the Israelites, preceding the Philistine penetration into the hill country precisely as claimed in Joshua 10:38, 39. However, more recently Israeli archaeologists have questioned whether Tell Beit Mirsim is Biblical Debir; and they have relocated it at *Khirbet Rabûd*, which was not destroyed at this time.[8]

Later, at Beitin, Biblical Bethel, Albright excavated a similar destruction in 1934 and connected it also with the incoming Israelites, invoking Joshua 8:12–17 and Judges 1:22–25. Then the British excavations began in 1936 at Lachish, described in Joshua 10:31 as having been destroyed by the Israelites. And, indeed, these excavations turned up evidence of a violent destruction in what the British designated as Level VI. The debris produced, among other things, fragments of a bowl inscribed in Egyptian hieratic script, badly broken but mentioning the "fourth year" of some king—in this case probably Merneptah, thus yielding a date of ca. 1230 B.C. (Today, the date would work out about 1210 B.C.) All along, Albright had argued against the traditional fifteenth century B.C. date for the Israelite settlement, preferring a date in the mid- to late thirteenth century B.C., and this appeared to be welcome confirmation.[9]

Not all the excavation of that period, however, could be construed to fit Albright's model. The most stunning exception was Jericho, the set piece of the book of Joshua and of the conquest theory. The German excavators Ernst Sellin and Carl Watzinger had dug there in 1907–9 and had concluded that Canaanite Jericho had been destroyed earlier—no later than 1600 B.C.—and there was therefore no city there in Joshua's day, even on the then-current "high chronology." In 1933–34, John Garstang, British Director of Antiquities in Palestine, returned to Jericho to test these conclusions, backed by funding from the well-known British conservative Sir Charles Marston. Garstang began by trying to move up the date of the destruction to the fifteenth century B.C., so as to suit the conventional date for Joshua. Then, when he discovered a great mud-brick city wall system that had collapsed outward in a fiery destruction, which he dated to the Late Bronze I period, just after 1500 B.C., he triumphantly announced that he had found the very city walls destroyed by Joshua and his men (Joshua 6:15–21). This dramatic "confirmation of Biblical history" quickly found its way into the press and into virtually all conservative handbooks and commentaries, where it is still sometimes repeated today. Unfortunately, in 1955–58 another eminent British archaeologist, the late Dame Kathleen Kenyon, returned to Jericho with vastly improved modern methods and demonstrated beyond any doubt that Garstang's city wall was destroyed ca. 2400 B.C.—nine hundred years earlier than Garstang claimed. Worse still, Kenyon confirmed that there simply was no Late Bronze occupation at Jericho after about 1350 B.C. and thus no occupation whatsoever at the site in Joshua's day.[10] (Of course, for some, that only made the Biblical story more miraculous than ever—Joshua destroyed a city that wasn't even there!) Albright had correctly opposed Garstang's interpretation and date all along, and now he quietly gave up Jericho as proof of the conquest model.

The excavations of the French archaeologist Judith Marquet-Krause in 1933–34 at et-Tell, Biblical ʿAi, proved no less embarrassing. Here also the major destruction was at the end of the Early Bronze Age, ca. 2400 B.C. And, in this case, the site was totally abandoned until sometime in the twelfth or eleventh century B.C., when a small Israelite village flourished on the centuries-old ruins. Despite the vivid, detailed account of the Israelite battle and capture of ʿAi in Joshua 7–8, there was simply no trace of an Israelite destruction, and indeed no Canaanite city there to be destroyed in Joshua's time. Albright, however, proposed an explanation for this state of affairs: the great destruction had actually taken place at Bethel a mile and a half away, but had understandably been fixed by later tradition at the prominent landmark of ʿAi, whose name in both Hebrew and Arabic means "ruin-heap." In short, Albright uncharacteristically adopted the Alt-Noth use of "aetiology"—a tale told to explain mysterious phenomena—to which we shall return below. Although undoubtedly ingenious, this suggestion was not accepted by many scholars, and recently it has been challenged again. A later American excavator of

ʿAi, J. A. Callaway, from Southern Baptist Theological Seminary, worked at the site from 1966 to 1973. He attempted to circumvent the negative evidence both by dating the Israelite conquest later than ca. 1200 B.C., and by supposing that "mainly it is a picture of political integration with the Iron I inhabitants of the land." But ʿAi remains a problem for any theory, just as Jericho does.[11]

The third major site of Joshua 1–10 is Gibeon, located at modern el-Jîb, six miles north-northwest of Jerusalem. This site was excavated in 1956–62 by J. B. Pritchard, who found that here again there was no evidence of a thirteenth-century B.C. occupation, much less the destruction of a fortified Late Bronze Age city. Thus the archaeological record is remarkably consistent in having produced totally negative evidence at all three of the sites prominently featured in the account of the central campaign of the Israelite "conquest" in Joshua 1–10:28.[12] (The excavation at Gibeon came almost too late for Albright's comment, but in any case Gibeon cannot be made to fit his hypothesis.)

Another later excavation, however, offered the best support yet for the conquest model. That was the work of Yigael Yadin and a team of Israeli archaeologists in 1955–58 at Tell el-Qedah in upper Galilee, clearly Biblical Hazor. Here it was found that the Late Bronze Age "lower city" (Stratum XIII)—a heavily occupied and strongly fortified citadel of some 180 acres, and the largest Bronze and Iron Age site in Palestine—was violently destroyed about 1200 B.C. The devastation was so severe that the entire "lower city" was abandoned thereafter and never again settled; there followed only a squatter occupation with some rubbish pits in the early twelfth century B.C. (Stratum XII), perhaps Israelite. Yadin quite naturally regarded his discoveries as confirmation of the Israelite victory claimed by Joshua 11:10–13 over Jabin, the king of Hazor, the most powerful Canaanite city state in the north—or, as the Bible puts it, "the head of all those kingdoms." Yadin's date of ca. 1230 B.C., based on the well-established cessation of Mycenaean ceramic imports around that time, agrees almost exactly with Albright's previous date for the Israelite destructions at Lachish and elsewhere.[13]

A final significant aspect of the effort of the first generation of archaeologists to place the Israelite conquest in historical perspective was the attempt to define Israelite *ethnicity*. How could one distinguish Israelite from Canaanite material culture? And if one could isolate uniquely Israelite elements in Iron I architectural styles, pottery, burial customs, and the like, might this yield a clue to whether the Israelites were newcomers, and if so, specify from where? Specifically, could archaeology say anything about either the nomadic or the Trans-Jordanian background from which, according to some interpretations of the evidence, the Israelites had emerged in Western Palestine?

Albright's principal contribution to this discussion was the notion that a type of collar-rim store jar found on many sites of the Iron I horizon was characteristically Israelite—what we would call today a type fossil of a particular culture. Albright also tried to show that the settlement of the sparsely occupied central hill country of Canaan was made possible by two other Israelite innovations: the development of the art of terrace farming, and the introduction of rock-cut plastered cisterns to conserve water in the long dry summer.[14] But Palestinian archaeology in the 1930s was still in its infancy, and the very difficult problem of recognizing diagnostic ethnic indicators in the archaeological record could not yet be dealt with effectively. Later, as we shall see, other scholars would attempt to see the incoming Israelites reflected in such new Iron I features as the "four-room house," and possibly in a certain style of bench tomb. But today, all these presuppositions concerning Israelite ethnicity must be re-examined.

Accumulating Evidence and Rival Views

I have thus far stressed the dominance in America of Albright and his followers, i.e., of the Biblical archaeology school. But I have also noted rival views, especially in Europe and in the more recent "Israeli school." Just as competing opinions about archaeological methods and interpretations arose over the issue of the historicity of the Patriarchs through the 1950s, so did they somewhat later over the even more crucial problem of the Israelite settlement in Canaan—especially as the archaeological evidence continued to accumulate rapidly in the postwar years. Let us briefly survey the scholarly scene up until about 1975.

Albright's mastery of Palestinian archaeology up until the 1960s was so surpassing that his conquest model persuaded many Biblical historians, especially in America. It is not surprising that he was followed closely by G. E. Wright, his chief protégé and later his successor as principal spokesman for American-style Biblical archaeology. Wright had already taken up Albright's earlier theme of archaeology and the Patriarchs, and now he addressed the issue of the Israelite conquest—characteristically as both Biblical scholar and practicing archaeologist. Already in 1940, in the third volume of the journal *The Biblical Archaeologist* (which Wright himself had founded in 1938), he had surveyed the growing archaeological evidence for what he termed "the epic of Conquest," closely following Albright's works of the same period. In Wright's literary critical analysis of Joshua 10 and Judges 1 in 1946, where he attempted to harmonize these contradictory accounts, and particularly in his 1957 textbook *Biblical Archaeology*, he developed his views further. Despite the embarrassment of Jericho and ʿAi, which Wright acknowledged but minimized, he declared: "We may safely conclude that during the thirteenth century a portion at least of the later nation of Israel gained entrance to Palestine by a carefully planned invasion."[15]

By the late 1950s the Albrightian synthesis—what the Germans had come to call the "American archaeological school's position"—had crystalized. This was seen clearly in the 1958 work of John Bright, *A History of Israel*, which for the past twenty-five years has been the most widely used textbook on the subject. Bright presents the views of Albright and Wright as foregone conclusions, stating that "When we come to the narratives of the conquest, the external [i.e., archaeological] evidence at our disposal is considerable and important. In the light of it, the historicity of such a conquest ought no longer to be denied."[16]

The last full-scale defense of the classic conquest model came in 1967, from Paul W. Lapp. Lapp was a Lutheran clergyman who had been a brilliant student of Albright and Wright at Johns Hopkins and Harvard and had gone on to become the director of the American School in Jerusalem. By the late 1960s (just before his death at 39) Lapp, always precocious, had begun to move tentatively away from traditional Biblical archaeology toward the "new archaeology." Nevertheless, in a 1969 article he still defended Albright's view of a pan-Israelite conquest. In a characteristically professional manner, Lapp cited much archaeological evidence and sharply opposed both the older "peaceful infiltration" model of the German school and the "peasant's revolt" model which was just then becoming popular (on which, more below). [17]

Meanwhile, following the establishment of the state of Israel in 1948 and during the rapid growth of the Israeli school, Albright's views were undergoing a similar evaluation. A number of Israeli scholars of conservative bent took his conquest model almost as a foregone conclusion. Yehezkiel Kaufmann's eight-volume *History of Israelite Religion* (issued in Hebrew from 1937 to 1956, and in English in 1960) totally rejected most modern literary critical theories and tended to read the Pentateuch quite literally as history. Kaufmann did accept the new, later dating of the conquest to the thirteenth century B.C., but his theological presuppositions (almost identical to those of some Protestant fundamentalists) made archaeology irrelevant—and indeed he quite consistently ignored it. His monograph, *The Biblical Account of the Conquest of Palestine* (1953), is a purely literary analysis of Joshua and Judges. Among Israeli archaeologists, S. Yeivin wrote a small book entitled *The Israelite Conquest of Canaan* in 1971, defending the conquest model, but this idiosyncratic work attracted little attention.

On the other hand, Israel's two leading archaeologists did address themselves to the subject in a significant way—especially the great soldier-statesman-scholar Yigael Yadin. His own excavations at Hazor in the 1950s had brought to light a most dramatic picture of a late thirteenth-century B.C. destruction, as we have seen—evidence that Yadin adduced again and again as dramatic confirmation of an Israelite conquest. He was opposed in this, however (as in virtually everything else), by his archrival, Yohanan Aharoni. Aharoni had conducted an extensive survey of early Israelite sites in upper Galilee for his doctoral dissertation, under Yadin, in 1957. Here he found numerous small unfortified villages established on virgin soil, characterized by poor architecture and degenerate pottery of the Late Bronze–Iron I transition. Later, Aharoni was able to use the evidence of other small village sites excavated in the 1960s and 1970s as support for a modified peaceful infiltration model. But his final view of the matter was that this phase of the Israelite settlement was as early as the fourteenth century B.C., followed by a phase of military campaigns by intruders in the mid- to late thirteenth century B.C. Aharoni's characterization of the settlement process as extremely complex was sound, but no one accepted his high dates—least of all Yadin. And today his confident identification of all the material culture remains (especially the so-called "conquest pottery") as Israelite is seen as simply begging the question.[18]

As early as the 1920s and 1930s, scholars in Germany had begun to develop their own distinctive approach to the problem of the Israelite settlement in Canaan, which we may call the "peaceful infiltration" model. This approach was based first on an advance beyond the earlier, purely literary criticism of the materials in Joshua-Judges, to a new analytical method called "form criticism" or "tradition history." Assuming with previous scholars the various documentary sources utilized by the later Biblical editors, the Germans, however, stressed the importance of the *Sitz im Leben*—the "life setting"—of each literary form of the Hebrew Bible, in this case the setting in the community and culture in which these conquest stories were preserved and handed down. In the German view, the stories of the fall of Jericho and ʿAi were "aeteological" legends, that is, artful tales told in order to explain to a later generation why things are the way they are. They were told to explain how Israel came to occupy the land, and especially to stress how these miraculous events were all proof of Israel's election and deliverance by Yahweh. Thus, for example, the story of ʿAi in Joshua has no historical basis at all, but is told simply to account for the famous landmark that many Israelites in the early Iron Age knew by sight, the great mound at ʿAi, whose Hebrew name actually means "ruin-heap." This, of course, neatly side-stepped the problem posed by the archaeologists' failure to find any trace of an Israelite destruction: there never had been one. Even Albright, as we have noted, was tempted by this "solution."

This "form critical" approach was pioneered in the works of the great German Biblical historian Albrecht Alt in the 1920s. But it was developed more fully by his pupil Martin Noth from the 1930s to the 1950s, especially in his programmatic work on textual studies, in commentaries on Numbers and Joshua, and in his great *History of Israel* (1958). The German school, despite its formidable work in literary criticism and in historical topography, never developed much interest in archaeology. Indeed, as Albright and his followers claimed, their negative attitude (Albright said "nihilism") was part of the reason for the strong controversy that would arise between the German and American schools from the 1930s through the early 1960s.

The second aspect of the German school's attack on the problem of the conquest was called "territorial history," or the study of regional settlement patterns over long periods of time. Here the fundamental treatment was Alt's brilliant 1925 essay, "The Settlement of the Israelites in Palestine." Alt utilized not only the newer analyses of the Biblical texts, but also the Amarna Letters and other historical documents, to show that the area settled by the Israelites in the Central Hills was precisely the portion of Canaan *not* heavily occupied in the preceding Late Bronze Age. From that Alt developed his notion of peaceful infiltration, the theory that the Israelites in the early Iron Age may indeed have been newcomers in certain regions, but they were more pastoral nomads in the process of becoming gradually sedentarized than they were conquerors. (This nomadic theory of Israelite origins—despite hints in the Hebrew Bible itself and many scholarly credentials—was to come under fire.) In Alt's view early stages of the Israelite penetration into the hill country did not threaten the old Late Bronze Age city-states along the coast and in the river valleys, much less displace the predominantly Canaanite population of Palestine. Alt acknowledged, however, a later stage of "territorial expansion," in which some Israelite raids may have been successfully carried out. In this way, the ambiguous archaeological evidence (always minimized in the German reconstructions) could be accommodated, and the apparently contradictory traditions in Joshua and Judges harmonized.

Alt was Europe's Albright—a scholar of enormous breadth and learning—and his views, continually developed up until his death in 1956, were widely influential in Biblical circles. But the solution of Alt and his disciples to the conquest-settlement problem seemed too radical to adherents of the American school, and moreover tended to ignore the progress of archaeology. Thus the two opposing schools battled it out well into the 1960s. The latest German restatements are by the Heidelberg professor Manfred Weippert, especially in his important and useful monograph, *The Settlement of the Israelite Tribes in Palestine* (1971). Here the newer archaeological evidence is indeed discussed, including that published in modern Hebrew, and a middle-of-the-road position is sought. But the basic differences in methodology of the two schools have still not been resolved, even to this day.[19]

Meanwhile, a novel approach was developing, again in America, that would challenge both the conquest and peaceful infiltration models. This view, the "peasants' revolt" model, was first articulated by G. E. Mendenhall in 1962 in a brief, seminal article that is one of the most original contributions to twentieth-century American Biblical scholarship. The peasants' revolt model derives largely from the application of sociological and anthropological methods to the study of early Israelite history. Mendenhall began by rejecting completely the German theories based on the idea of a nomadic origin for the Israelites. He found no real evidence of such a background in the historical memories as preserved in the Hebrew Bible. Furthermore, he was able to show from both ancient textual and modern ethnographic evidence that most concepts of nomads—i.e., as completely unsettled, barbarian invaders—were romantic fancies based on false analogies with modern camel-mounted Beduins. Mendenhall then argued that the ancient Hebrews of the Bible were to be identified rather with the 'Apiru of the fourteenth-century B.C. Amarna Letters from Palestine (noted above). Not only were their names etymologically similar, so were their socio-economic roles: both were outcasts, free-booters, landless peasants, dropouts from the increasingly corrupt urban Canaanite culture of the Late Bronze Age of the fourteenth and thirteenth centuries B.C. In Mendenhall's words:

> both the Amarna materials and the biblical events represent politically the same process: namely, the withdrawal, not physically but geographically and subjectively, of large population groups from any obligation to the existing political regimes, and therefore, the renunciation of any protection from those sources. In other words, there was no statistically important invasion of Palestine at the beginning of the twelve tribe system of Israel. There was no radical displacement of population, there was no genocide,

there was no large-scale driving out of population, only of royal administrators (of necessity!). In summary, there was no real conquest of Palestine at all; what happened instead may be termed, from the point of view of the secular historian interested only in socio-political processes, a peasants' revolt against the network of interlocking Canaanite city states.

Although he did not develop the idea fully until somewhat later (1973), Mendenhall sought the impetus for the emergence of later Israel as a distinct and cohesive ethnic group in a radically new religious and political ideology. He called this the "rule of Yahweh," expressed in the Bible in the idea of covenant relations between God and people, as well as between individuals.

Despite many fresh and provocative insights, one of the crucial weaknesses of Mendenhall's argument was that he could not define Israelite ethnicity in terms of material culture, i.e., archaeologically (or, for that matter, in political or sociological terms). Nor could he correlate events of the supposed peasants' revolt with the actual stratigraphic sequence of the Late Bronze Age sites in Palestine. Indeed, Mendenhall largely ignored the archaeological record, which shows no real cultural breaks in the fourteenth and thirteenth centuries B.C., but does witness a major upheaval at many sites later, around 1200 B.C.[20]

Mendenhall's sociological approach to the question of Israelite origins was provocative enough not only to survive but eventually to launch a new movement in Biblical scholarship. The maturing of this trend is seen in the massive 1979 treatment of Norman K. Gottwald, *The Tribes of Yahweh: A Sociology of the Religion of Liberated Israel, 1250–1050 B.C.E.*, which is probably the most important book to appear in Biblical (OT) studies in the past twenty years. Gottwald's nine-hundred-page, very closely reasoned analysis is impossible to reduce to a paragraph, but his salient points are as follows. He subjects both the conquest and peaceful infiltration models to an exhaustive, and in my mind compelling, critique. His own preference is for a much expanded and more systematic application of Mendenhall's revolt model. Gottwald explains the emergence of Israel in the twentieth century B.C. as due to an "anti-statist" tribal revolt of depressed peasants in the Canaanite countryside—what he terms an "egalitarian socio-economic movement." "Yahwism," the religion of early Israel, was the symbolic expression of this social revolution. Because Gottwald is taking (in part) a functionalist approach to religion, he tries to define both the material and social consequences of Israelite ethnicity, looking at such societal features as adaptation to the natural environment, agricultural practices, technology, and economy. Here he draws heavily on the theory of the new archaeology, as well as the little pertinent archaeological evidence available in the mid-1970s.

Gottwald's unabashed "historical-cultural-material" program of research has been criticized by some as simply Marxist economic determinism projected upon ancient Israel. His approach, however, is more congenial than that of any other contemporary Biblical scholar to the agenda of the new archaeology. I believe that Gottwald's brief statement in his preface should serve as the new slogan for the cooperation of our two disciplines in future: "Only as the full *materiality* of ancient Israel is more securely grasped will we be able to make proper sense of its *spirituality*."[21]

New Data: Possibilities for a Synthesis?

We must now bring the story up to date, first by sketching the rich new archaeological data—not available to Gottwald just ten years ago—and then by outlining the possibilities for a new synthesis that will go beyond all current models for the Israelite settlement.

First, let us summarize the vast accumulation of archaeological evidence since the formulation of the classic conquest model by Wright and Albright, who had only a handful of sites to work with. The newer evidence has not been surveyed *in toto* by any Palestinian archaeologist since 1967 and is inaccessible to most Biblical historians.[22] Given the bulk of the material, I have found it necessary to reduce it to the following tables, which summarize the stratigraphic sequence at virtually all known Late Bronze–early Iron I sites in Palestine and Trans-Jordan, published and unpublished, correlated with the pertinent Biblical references in Numbers, Joshua, and Judges.

TABLE I
Biblical references and archaeological evidence concerning Canaanite sites claimed to have been taken by the Israelites (Late Bronze–early Iron I)

Site	References[a]	Biblical remarks	Archaeological evidence
Zepath/Hormah	Numbers 21:1–3; Judges 1:17	Destroyed	No LB occupation (if the site's identification with Tel Masos is correct)
Jericho	Judges 6:1–21;	Destroyed	No LB II occupation
ʿAi	Joshua 8:24	Destroyed	No LB II occupation
Bethel	Joshua 8:17; Judges 1:22–28	Destroyed	Destruction at the end of LB II
Jerusalem	Joshua 10:1–27; Judges 1:8, 21	Texts contradictory	LB II occupation, but no evidence of destruction
Libnah	Joshua 10:29, 31	Destroyed	Tentatively identified with Tell es-Sâfi
Lachish	Joshua 10:31	Destroyed	Level VI destroyed ca. 1150 B.C.
Hebron	Joshua 14:13–15, 15:13, 14; Judges 1:10	Texts imply that the city was taken, but no destruction is described.	No evidence
Debir	Joshua 10:38, 39, 15:17; Judges 1:11–13	Destroyed	Identification uncertain. If the site is Tell Beit Mirsim, then there is evidence of destruction; if Tell Rabûd, no evidence of destruction.
Makkedah	Joshua 10:28	Destroyed	No LB occupation (if the site's identification with Kh. el-Qôm is correct)
Eglon	Joshua 10:34, 35	Destroyed	No evidence of destruction (if the tentative identification of the site as Tell el-Hesi is correct)

TABLE I (*continued*)

Site	References[a]	Biblical remarks	Archaeological evidence
Hazor	Joshua 11:10–13	Destroyed, but later mentioned as still existing	Lower City, gnl. Stratum XIII, violently destroyed ca. 1200 B.C.
Dan	Judges 18:11–28	Destroyed	Definite LB II occupation; unclear evidence concerning destruction at end of LB II
Gaza	Judges 1:18	Taken	No evidence
Ashkelon	Judges 1:18	Taken	No evidence
Ekron	Judges 1:18	Taken	No evidence
Heshbon	Numbers 21:25–30	Destroyed	No LB II occupation
Dibon	Numbers 21:30	Implied destroyed	No. LB II occupation
Medeba	Numbers 21:30	Implied destroyed	No evidence

[a]References are to the Revised Standard Version of the Bible.

TABLE 2
Biblical references and archaeological evidence concerning sites reportedly spared
destruction by the Israelites

Site	References[a]	Biblical remarks	Archaeological evidence
Gibeon	Joshua 9:16; Judges 11:9	Absorbed by treaty into the Israelite confederacy	Scant LB II occupation; no destruction
Beth-shan	Judges 1:27	King killed; city not destroyed	LB II Stratum VI not destroyed
Ta‘anach	Judges 1:27; 12:21	Not destroyed	No LB IIb occupation, but evidence of twelfth-century B. C. reoccupation (Ia-b)
Dor	Judges 1:27, 12:23	King killed; city not destroyed	No evidence
Ibleam	Judges 1:27	Not destroyed	No evidence
Megiddo	Judges 1:27, 12:21	King killed; city not destroyed	LB II Stratum VIIb-a continues into Iron I
Akko	Judges 1:31	Not destroyed	No evidence
Achziv	Judges 1:31	Not destroyed	No evidence
Rehob	Judges 1:31	Not destroyed	No evidence
Beth-shemesh	Judges 1:33	Not destroyed; inhabitants enslaved	LB II Stratum IVb destroyed
Gezer	Joshua 10:33, 12:12	King killed; no mention of destruction	Stratum XIV destroyed by Philistines; became Israelite in the tenth century B.C.
Shechem	Joshua 24; Judges 9	Came into the Israelite confederation by treaty	LB II continues into the twelfth century B.C. without interruption

[a]References are to the Revised Standard Version of the Bible.

TABLE 3
Sites destroyed ca. 1200 B.C., but not mentioned in the Bible

Site	Archaeological evidence
Tell Abu Hawam	Identification unknown; LB II Stratum Vc destroyed, probably by "Sea Peoples"
Tell Qashish	Identification unknown; LB II destruction
Tel Yoqneam	Biblical Yoqneam; some LB II destruction (Stratum VII)
Tel Yin'am	Identification unknown; LB II occupation, some destruction at end (Stratum VIb)
Tell el-Far'ah N.	Biblical Tirzah, possible destruction at end of LB II
Aphek	Biblical Aphek; LB II destruction, perhaps by "Sea Peoples"
Jaffa	Biblical Joppa; some LB II destruction of Stratum IV
Ashdod	Biblical Ashdod; LB II Stratum XIV destroyed, undoubtedly by "Sea Peoples"
Tel Mor	Identification unknown, LB II Stratum 7 ends in destruction
Tell es-Sharia	Possibly Biblical Ziklag; Stratum IX destroyed ca. 1150, possibly by "Sea Peoples"
Tell el-Far'ah S.	Biblical Sharuhen?; some disturbance, Philistine tombs in early twelfth century
Deir 'Allā	Identification unknown; LB II "sanctuary" destroyed, site reoccupied in twelfth century

We can summarize the information in these tables in several ways. First, of a total of sixteen sites clearly said by the Bible to have been destroyed, only three have produced archaeological evidence for a destruction ca. 1200 B.C.: Bethel, Lachish, and Hazor. This is virtually the same evidence adduced by Albright and Wright a generation ago; we can add only the newer data from Lachish for changing Albright's 1230 B.C. date to ca. 1175–50 B.C. Of the remaining thirteen sites, seven claimed by the Bible as Israelite destructions either were not even occupied in the period, or show no trace of a destruction. Finally, for six of these sixteen Biblical sites, archaeology is simply silent: they have not been positively located, or they have not yet been excavated sufficiently to yield evidence.

Second, if we look at the picture the other way around, of the twelve sites said by the Bible *not* to have been destroyed by the Israelites (mostly in Judges 1), five have been excavated and indeed show no destruction ca. 1200 B.C. The other six either have not been dug or have produced evidence that is inconclusive.

Finally, there are at least twelve other Late Bronze–Iron I sites of this horizon, either unidentified or not mentioned by name in the Bible. Of these, six were destroyed in all likelihood by the Philistines or "Sea Peoples" and one by the Egyptian Pharaoh Merneptah (above). The other six were destroyed by unknown agents—perhaps one or two of them by the Israelites, although there is no Biblical tradition to that effect and no way of ascertaining archaeologically the identity of the destroyers.

In conclusion, it may be stated confidently that the archaeological evidence today is overwhelmingly against the classic conquest model of Israelite origins, as envisioned in the book of Joshua and in much Biblical scholarship until recently. Many Late Bronze–Iron I sites were not destroyed at all; of those that were, more must be attributed to the Philistines or to unknown causes than to any groups to be identified as Israelite. On the other hand, there is virtually no archaeological support for peaceful infiltration or nomadic models, either. There is nothing whatsoever in the archaeological record to suggest that any elements in the Iron I population of Palestine (except, of course, the Philistines) had either a pastoral-nomadic background or extra-Palestinian origins. As we shall now see, the peasants' revolt model and the accounts of the book of Judges fare much better in the light of both recent archaeological discoveries and textual analysis.

In the last decade or so, American and Israeli archaeologists have suddenly brought to light evidence far more exciting and instructive than the presence or absence of Late Bronze destruction layers at the major tells, or mounds, of Palestine. This consists of the discovery and excavation of at least half a dozen one-period sites that we may regard as "early Israelite" villages of the twelfth and eleventh centuries B.C.—the first such evidence we have had. All are still largely unpublished, but preliminary reports clarify the general picture. (See figure 1.)

In the late 1960s and early 1970s J. A. Callaway excavated the small, hilltop village of et-Tell, Biblical ʿAi, ten miles north-northeast of Jerusalem, near Bethel (figure 2). Although, as we have already noted, there was absolutely no Late Bronze Canaanite occupation at the site, Callaway did find a twelfth- or eleventh-century B.C. village. This unwalled village consisted of some twenty distinctive "four-room" pillared courtyard houses of a type often characterized as Israelite (see figure 22 and the description on page 102), each possessing one or more rock-hewn cisterns (figure 3). Callaway thus estimates that ʿAi had a population of about a hundred and fifty, but if there remain other unexcavated houses filling the entire area, then there could have been a population twice that size. The pottery repertoire at ʿAi was limited and consisted mostly of cooking pots, a distinctive "collar-rim" store jar, and other vessels derived from Late Bronze Age Canaanite types of the late thirteenth century B.C. One house contained a metal-working hearth with a bronze chisel and a dagger. The two brief phases of occupation came to an end with some evidence of a destruction about 1050 B.C., or roughly during the rise of Saul at the beginning of the United Monarchy.[23]

Between 1969 and the middle 1970s, Callaway and his colleague Robert Coolley cleared a similar unfortified village, at Kh. Raddana (ancient Beeroth?), just on the outskirts of Ramallah north of Jerusalem, in an area of heavily terraced hillsides (figure 4). Here there were only six courtyard houses, each with one or more cisterns, arranged around a number of open work and storage areas, some with hearths and silos (figure 5). The size and arrangement would suggest a tiny hamlet occupied by

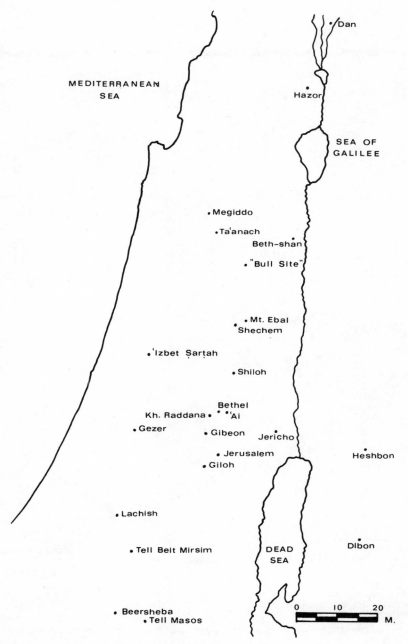

Figure 1. Key sites of the period of the early Israelite settlement in Canaan.

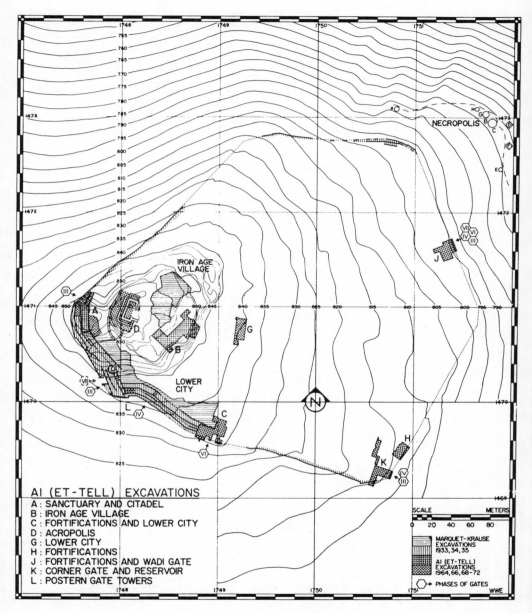

Figure 2. Top plan of ʿAi, showing the various excavation areas; note Area B, the early Israelite village. From Callaway, *The Early Bronze Age Sanctuary at Ai (et-Tell)*, fig. 3.

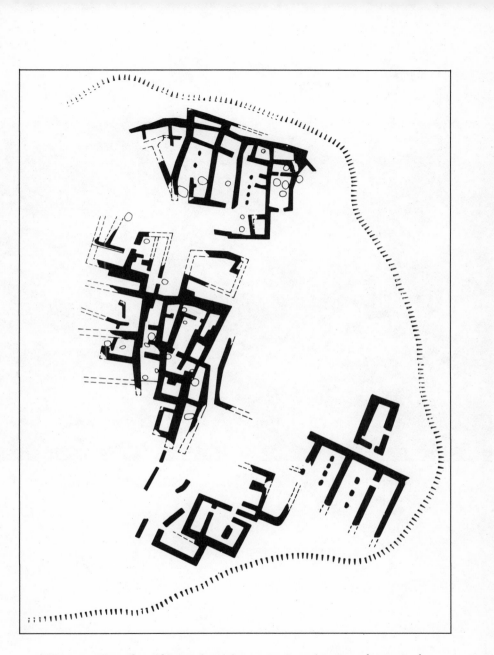

Figure 3. Plan of twelfth- to eleventh-century B.C. houses and courtyards
at ʿAi. From Katzenstein et al., *The Architecture of Ancient Israel from the Pre-
historic to the Roman Periods*, p. 199.

Figure 4. The hilltop site of Kh. Raddana; photo by W. G. Dever.

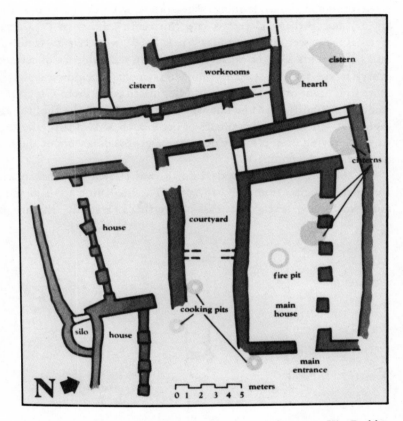

Figure 5. Plan of twelfth- eleventh-century B.C. houses at Kh. Raddana. From J. A. Callaway, *BAR* 9, no. 9:47.

an extended family (or small "clan") of thirty to forty people, subsisting on herding and terrace farming. The pottery was nearly identical to that of ʿAi, but perhaps closer to late thirteenth-century B.C. Canaanite styles. One vessel was a peculiar "trick bowl" with twenty handles and bull head spouts at the rim. Here, too, there was evidence of cottage industry in the form of several bronze implements, including an axe. The most significant object was a jar handle, inscribed in Proto-Canaanite and reading "Aḥilu[d]," a name known from the period of the Biblical judges (figure 6). There were two phases of occupation at Raddana, the site apparently having been partially destroyed and abandoned about the middle of the eleventh century B.C.[24]

Tel Masos (possibly Biblical Hormah) was cleared by German and Israeli archaeologists from 1972 to 1975. The small Iron I village is in the northern Negev, seven miles east of Beersheba. Happily, the first of its

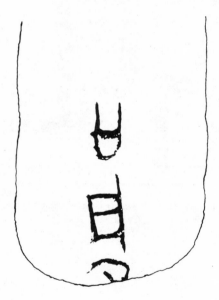

Figure 6. The inscribed jar handle from Kh. Raddana
(late thirteenth or early twelfth century B.C.). From J.
A. Callaway and R. E. Cooley, *BASOR* 201, fig. 2.

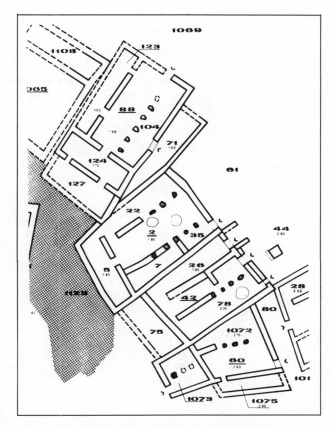

Figure 7. Plan of Str. 11b–a courtyard houses at Tel Masos (eleventh century B.C.). From V. Fritz and A. Kempinski, *Ergebnisse der Ausgrabungen auf der Ḥirbet el-Mšaš (Tēl Māśōś)*, plate 3.

three strata was clearly dated by a scarab of Seti II (ca. 1198–92 B.C.). The fifteen-acre village was founded on the relatively rich loessal soil of this region of low rolling hills, the Biblical Negev. The earliest occupation (Stratum III), consisting at first only of squatter dwellings (111b), then later of flimsy courtyard houses (111a) with rather poor early Iron I pottery and storage pits, was evidently Israelite. It began just before 1200 B.C. and ended in a destruction perhaps a century later. Stratum 11b-a, with better four-room houses (figure 7) and much finer pottery—including northern imports and "Midianite" wares—may indicate either

a Philistine takeover or, more likely, continued Israelite occupation during the *Pax Philistina*. About 950 B.C. there was again a destruction.
Stratum I was subsequently founded and lasted until it was abandoned
ca. 800 B.C.

Of prime importance here is the fact that Tel Masos III may be the
site of the small, unwalled early Israelite village of Hormah (figure 8).
Its inhabitants were newcomers, at least to this region, and they may have
been pastoral nomads settling down; the animal bones retrieved show that

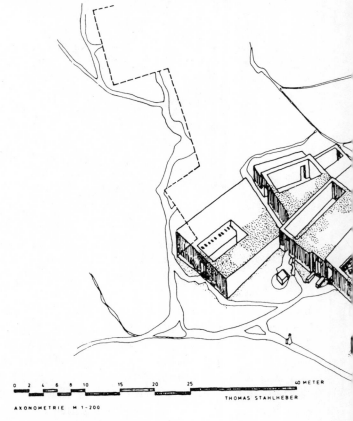

Figure 8. An artist's reconstruction of part of the Str. III village at Tel
Masos (twelfth century B.C.). Fritz and Kempinski, fig. 2.

they herded sheep, goats, and cattle for a livelihood. Certainly the Israelite villagers had contact with local Canaanite culture, as both pottery and house forms indicate. Yet the site is not built on or even near any destroyed Late Bronze Age city, as Numbers 21:1–3 implies, but was rather founded peacefully in the open countryside, on virgin soil. The site area was large enough for as many as a hundred and thirty houses; this suggests a population estimate of up to nine hundred, yet even half that figure seems too high.[25]

The site of ʿIzbet Ṣarṭah, probably to be identified as Biblical Ebenezer, was almost completely excavated by the Israeli archaeologists Moshe Kochavi, Israel Finkelstein, and others (1976–78). The site is two miles east of the large Middle to Late Bronze mound of Aphek at the northern

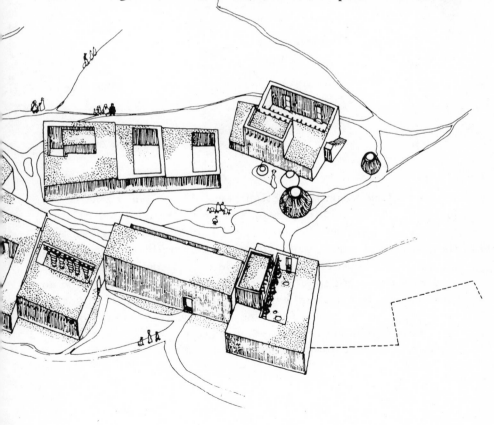

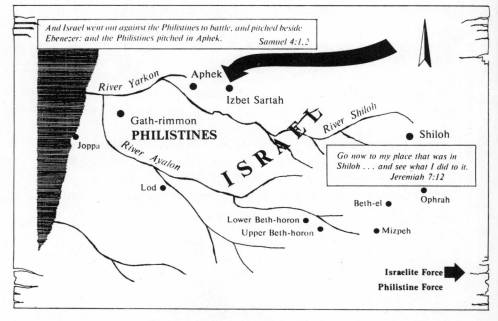

And Israel went out against the Philistines to battle, and pitched beside Ebenezer: and the Philistines pitched in Aphek.   Samuel 4:1,2

Go now to my place that was in Shiloh . . . and see what I did to it. Jeremiah 7:12

Israelite Force
Philistine Force

Figure 9. The location of ʿIzbet Ṣarṭah (Ebenezer) in relation to the Philistine plain. From M. Kochavi and A. Demsky, *BAR* 4, no. 3:20.

periphery of the Shephelah-Philistine plain—in the "buffer zone" at the juncture with the foothills (figure 9). Stratum III, occupied from ca. 1200 to 1150 B.C., yielded a picture of several crude courtyard houses with silos, inside a perimeter wall. Stratum II, very briefly occupied around 1025 B.C. after a century-long gap, produced a fine four-room house with numerous stone-lined silos (figure 10). In one of the silos was found an ostracon (inscribed potsherd) written in the Proto-Canaanite script of the century B.C. or so. It was a five-line abecedary, or schoolboy's practice text, with the Canaanite-Hebrew alphabet (figure 11). Stratum I represents a final brief occupation around 1000 to 950 B.C., early in the Israelite Monarchy.

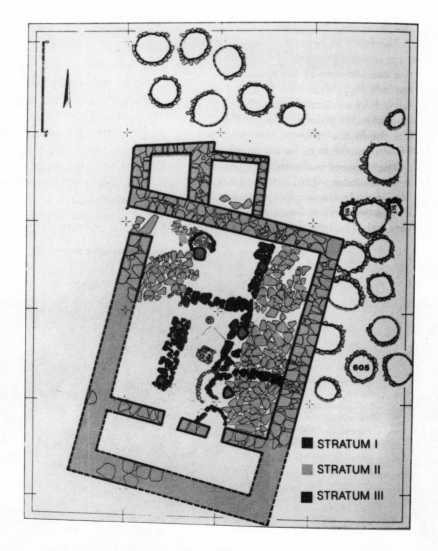

STRATUM I
STRATUM II
STRATUM III

Figure 10. Str. II courtyard house and silos at ʿIzbet Ṣarṭah (eleventh century B.C.). From A. Demsky and M. Kochavi, *BAR* 4, no. 3:26.

There are three particularly significant facts about ʿIzbet Ṣarṭah: the site's location near a large Canaanite town, with, however, a distinct social structure and agrarian economy; the progression in the twelfth and eleventh centuries from herding to intensive agriculture, and from poor to better housing; and the evidence in the ostracon of both continuity with Canaanite culture and widespread literacy. In Finkelstein's view the early Israelite settlers at Ebenezer were former pastoral nomads who migrated from the east, possibly to be identified with the "house of Joseph" of the Hebrew Bible. It must be stressed, however, that there is no material evidence of such migrations; and indeed the ʿIzbet Ṣarṭah pottery is virtually identical to that at nearby Gezer, a site which was certainly not Israelite in the twelfth and eleventh centuries B.C., according to either archaeology or Biblical tradition.[26]

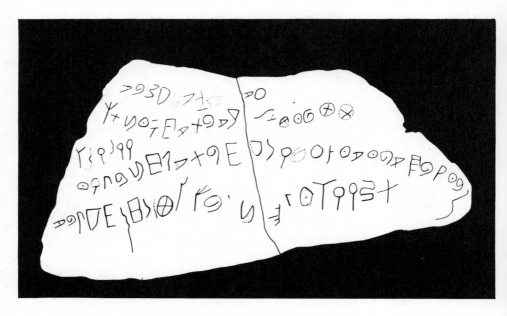

Figure 11. Proto-Canaanite abecedary of Str. II at ʿIzbet Ṣarṭah (twelfth century B.C.). From A. Demsky and M. Kochavi, *BAR* 4, no. 3:22.

Our last village is Giloh, five miles southwest of Jerusalem, near Beth-lehem, excavated by Amihai Mazar (1978–79). This is a tiny fortified hill-top site (possibly Biblical Ba'al Perazim), with only fragmentary remains of a few courtyard houses (figure 12). The pottery, however, is the most extensively published thus far from one of these early Israelite villages (figure 13). It is clearly transitional Late Bronze II/Iron I and can be dated precisely to ca. 1200 B.C.; it is demonstrably in the degenerate Canaanite tradition, but there are a few new elements that clearly place this pottery in the early Iron I tradition. This does not necessarily mean, however, that the inhabitants of Giloh were pastoral nomads settling down, much less newcomers to central Palestine. Mazar's analysis—the best balanced and most authoritative statement yet by an archaeologist—concludes with this very sensible statement:

> Archaeology can provide positive evidence for the phase of establishing new sites in regions previously unsettled, but it cannot supply evidence for a possible nomadic phase which may have preceded the settlement; it gives a clue to the destruction of some major Canaanite cities which probably happened as a result of military conflicts between the Israelites and the Canaanite population, yet it cannot be taken as proof of a total, "monolithic" conquest. Thus the variety of the archaeological finds illustrates the complex process of the Israelite conquest and settlement.[27]

In addition to excavating new one-period sites in central Palestine, Is-raeli archaeologists in the last decade or so have been concentrating on region-by-region topographical surveys. These have turned up hundreds of new Iron I sites, many of them probably founded by the Israelites. These surface surveys actually began with Aharoni's work in the 1950s in upper Galilee, noted above. The Institute of Archaeology at Tel Aviv University, founded by Aharoni in 1968, has continued these surveys, first in the Negev, the coastal plain, and into lower Galilee; then after 1967 in the West Bank. In the latter region, the heartland of ancient Ephraim and Manasseh, the unpublished surveys of Israel Finkelstein and Adam Zertal are especially important. Finkelstein, for instance, has dis-covered no less than 409 sites to the east of 'Izbet Ṣarṭah up as far as the Jerusalem hills, of which more than 75 were founded in Iron I. In

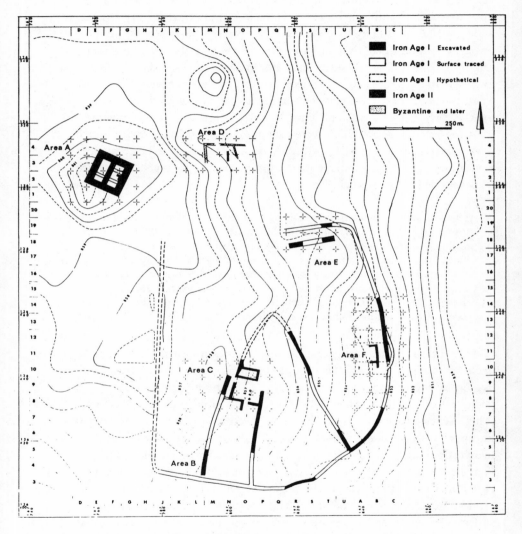

Figure 12. Plan of Giloh, showing remains of various periods.
From A. Mazar, *IEJ* 31, fig. 2.

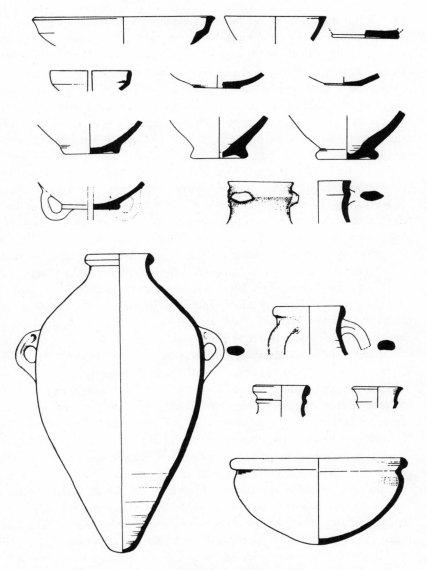

Figure 13. Early Iron Age/"Israelite" pottery from Giloh. From A. Mazar, *IEJ* 31, fig. 9.

the central hill country as a whole, according to Lawrence Stager, recent surveys have shown that the number and density of permanent settlements increased dramatically just after 1200 B.C.: from 23 Late Bronze sites to 114 Iron I sites (97 of the latter founded during Iron I). Individual Late Bronze settlements were larger (median size 21 to 31 acres) than those of Iron I (median size 2 to 3 acres), yet the total *occupied* area was only about 175 acres, compared with the roughly 475 acres occupied during Iron I—an increase the demographers can hardly attribute to natural growth alone.[28]

From the foregoing it is obvious that there was a sizeable influx of new people into the highland zone of Canaan, beginning in the early twelfth century B.C. I believe that we may tentatively identify these newcomers as "Israelites," as a few archaeologists and Biblical historians have already suggested. But this conclusion leaves critical questions to consider: Can we offer any tangible evidence for this identification, on which so much rests? That is, can we detect "Israelite" ethnicity in the archaeological record? Who were these early Israelites, and where did they come from?

I shall now outline a possible synthesis, drawing on the recent excavations and surveys just described, as well as on current research using the insights of the newer, interdisciplinary archaeology. Already it is possible to specify the distinguishing characteristics of what may be termed "Israelite"—or perhaps better, "Proto-Israelite"—society.

To begin with, the typical early Israelite sites are mostly in the central regions of Palestine, especially the hill country, and not on destroyed or deserted Late Bronze sites (where they had previously been sought), but founded in the early twelfth century B.C. Most are small, unwalled villages, characterized by early four-room courtyard houses, rock-hewn cisterns, and silos—all features typical of the material culture of agrarian or peasant societies. The economy is based on small-scale terrace farming, with some herding of livestock and primitive cottage industries, but also with some evidence for trade with more distant urban centers. The social structure, unlike that of the urban Late Bronze Age, appears to be socially undifferentiated in the extreme, although we already have evidence of fairly widespread literacy among groups that may have been elites. The pottery, however—in contrast to the newly introduced house forms, distinctive socio-economic structure, and settlement patterns—is solidly in the LB IIB Canaanite tradition; nearly all forms exhibit only the expected, normal development from the thirteenth into the twelfth (and even eleventh) centuries B.C. There is no evidence whatsoever in the material culture to suggest that the Israelites originated outside Palestine, or that more than an insignificant number of them came from a pastoral nomadic background. Finally, most of these early Iron I sites were abandoned by the end of the eleventh century B.C. or before, with the growth of a more concentrated urban population at the beginning of the Monarchy.

The inescapable conclusion—only likely to be enhanced by future archaeological research[29]—is that the Israelite settlement in Canaan was part of the larger transition from the Late Bronze to the Iron Age. It was a gradual, exceedingly complex process, involving social, economic, and political—as well as religious—change, with many regional variations.

If this is so, then recent archaeological discoveries are most compatible with the peasants' revolt model—although, of course, they cannot prove this model. In any case, they cannot any longer be construed as supporting nomadic infiltration, much less conquest models, as previous scholars had maintained. It must be stressed that in the light of archaeology today, it is the Late Bronze–Iron I continuity in material culture—not the discontinuity—that is striking, the more so as research progresses. In other words, of the two Biblical accounts, Joshua and Judges, the latter is by far the more realistic and thus more historically reliable, because it relates the emergence of Israel to the actual, conventional process of socio-economic change that we can document in Palestine on this horizon. Also, the frank recognition in Judges of syncretism in early Israelite religion—of the pervasive influence of the old fertility cults of Canaan—instills further confidence in this account. In human terms, we must conclude that it was not so much in a suprahistorical ideology that Israel was born, but in the actual, daily, life-or-death conflict with Canaanite religion and culture. Yahwism was not "handed down from heaven" to Moses, an immutable spiritual ideal; it was worked out in bitter experience on the soil of Canaan, in constant tension and dialogue with Israel's pagan neighbors (as I shall show in the final chapter). The surprising thing was that Israel survived, and indeed finally eclipsed the long-established sophisticated cultures of Canaan, both materially and spiritually. In the end, the "peasants" triumphed and are remembered still for their struggle, while their Canaanite overlords vanished and are forgotten.

But we still have not managed to specify just how the ancient Israelites were different culturally—the question already raised concerning how archaeological evidence may define ethnicity. The material culture of the early Israelite highland villages sketched above exhibits the following cultural traits: four-room courtyard houses; early iron technology and implements; collar-rim store jars and a few other distinctive ceramic forms; developed terrace farming; stone silos; plastered cisterns; distinctive bench style tombs; and open-air shrines, rather than temples. While these features may indeed be typical of supposed Israelite sites in the twelfth century B.C., they are not exclusively so, nor are they necessarily Israelite innovations, as often thought. Some of these characteristics are now found in non-Israelite areas such as Trans-Jordan, and in earlier Canaanite contexts going well back into the Late Bronze Age. It appears that the distinctive combination of those elements is not so much "Israelite" as it is a diagnostic feature of the early Iron Age cultures of Palestine generally, especially in the rural and highland areas.

More significant than individual traits, however, are such cultural factors as settlement patterns, economic structure, and social organization of Israelite heartland villages. One of the most promising applications of the new archaeology to the Israelite settlement horizon is that of Lawrence Stager, who utilizes the recent excavations and surveys discussed above, plus the Biblical texts, together with studies of settlement patterns, house forms, demography, technology, economy, and ethnography.[30] Stager's very sophisticated interdisciplinary analysis has demonstrated that the small architectural units, the agrarian economy, and the egalitarian social structure can be directly compared with Biblical descriptions of tribal life in the period of the Judges. In texts in Joshua and Judges there are numerous architectural terms that, when re-examined in the light of archaeology, can be connected to actual dwellings that we now have. More important, the individual Iron I courtyard house, a typical peasant farmhouse, can be related to the Biblical *bet ha-āv*, usually translated literally as "house of the father," but in sociological terms a descent group or "nuclear family." And the clusters of these houses at the sites we have surveyed then reflects the Biblical *mišpāḥ*ah, to be understood as an extended or multiple family. Thus Stager concludes that these early Iron I highland sites are Israelite "kin-based villages," of precisely the type described in the Bible (figure 14). This approach yields the best evidence yet that the new archaeology can indeed deal with the difficult problem of ethnicity. We can now begin to say specifically how Israelites differed from Canaanites in their material culture and social organization, and yet at the same time stress the Late Bronze–Iron I continuity that is increasingly clear in the archaeological record.

Although archaeology may be successful in recognizing the "material correlates" of human behavior and social organization, it reaches its limitations when it comes to ideology. Archaeology does not yet, and probably cannot, comment on the political or religious motivations behind the emergence of ancient Israel. We may tend to agree that Yahwism, whether a revolutionary social movement or not, was probably the driving force. But we cannot define Yahwism archaeologically beyond describing religious practice (see chapter 4). We can only say that in the cultural vacuum following the collapse of Canaanite society in the twelfth century B.C., there arose in central Palestine a new ethnic consciousness and solidarity. The emergence of this ethnicity need not have been accompanied by a revolt at all; it may be viewed rather as simply a normal and even predictable historical development in the evolution of a complex society. Archaeology may provide an ecology in which socio-economic change becomes explicable, but it cannot explain the ultimate derivation of that change. That may be a task for theology.

Conclusion

We began by noting the phenomenon of the emergence of Israel in Canaan around 1200 B.C., a process which, although the very foundation of Biblical history and religion, was absolutely unattested outside the Bible until a hundred years ago. What can we now conclude?

Certainly archaeology has illuminated the settlement process brilliantly

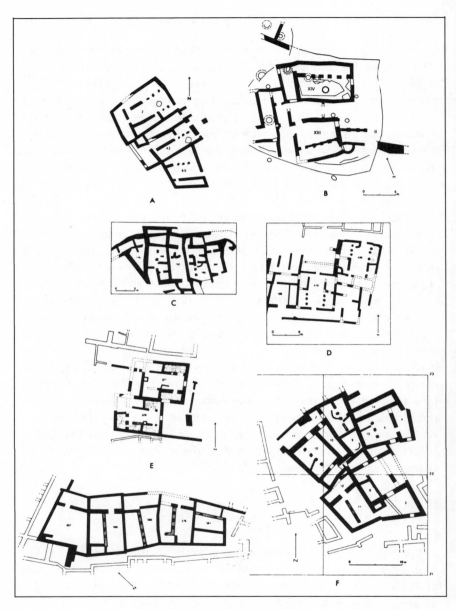

Figure 14. Examples of Iron Age "Israelite" house plans: A, Tel Masos;
B, Kh. Raddana; C. ʿAi; D, Tell el-Farʿah (N); E, Tell el-Farʿah (N); F, Tell
Beit Mirsim. From L. E. Stager, *BASOR* 260, Fig. 9.

through both textual and artifactural discoveries—but not in the way the earlier Biblical archaeologists expected. Rather than simply confirming an Israelite military conquest of Canaan under Joshua, or documenting the sedentarization of incoming nomads from the desert, archaeology has forced upon us a totally new way of looking at early Israel. The admittedly radical view of Israel as a "peasants' revolt" (in Gottwald and a number of other contemporary Biblical scholars) has been powerfully buttressed by the new interdisciplinary archaeology—so much so that we have undoubtedly reached a crucial turning point in scholarship. If this view is correct, then there never was a statistically significant conquest of Palestine at all. Perhaps only the House of Joseph was ever in Egypt; the other "tribes" of Israel were probably local Canaanite groups (like the Gibeonites and the Shechemites), who joined the Israelite tribal confederation by covenant and thus became Yahwists, as the Bible implies in some cases. There was of necessity some armed conflict with the Canaanite city-states, but for the most part the emergence of early Israel was the consequence of an ideological revolution, with distinctive socio-economic effects that are reflected in the archaeological record.

Must we conclude then that the Bible was wrong? That the Pentateuch and the Book of Joshua have no historical basis? Not necessarily. As scholars have long known, this lengthy epic narrative—the major part of the Deuteronomic history—was not compiled until the seventh century B.C., and the version that we now have in the Hebrew Bible did not take final form before the post-Exilic period in the fourth century B.C. The Deuteronomic historiography was obviously a late construct, a theological one which deliberately overemphasized the themes of the exodus from Egypt, the holy war, and the covenant as extensions of the "promised land" motif.[31] Nevertheless, the Deuteronomist also preserved earlier materials with alternative views, such as portions of Judges. What recent research has done is simply to retrieve one neglected strand of the complex Biblical narratives concerning Israel's origins. The real contribution of modern archaeology has been to provide for the first time, alongside the theological explanation, a sociological setting that makes it possible to see the settlement process in a new light. The Biblical writers were aware of the social setting, of course, but they were more concerned with viewing history as the *magnalia dei*, the "mighty acts of God." For us moderns, however, who have known so many peasants' revolts in the twentieth century, the current sociological model may be more relevant, because it leads to a greater comprehension of ancient Israel in all its diversity and vitality, as well as to a more profound appreciation of its dynamic relation to Canaanite religion and culture.

Finally, the new stress on the humanity of Israel need not depreciate the divine element—that is, faith. Ultimately, the Biblical writers faced the same problem we do: how to account for the unique reality of the people of Israel. They fell back on the only analogy they had, historical experience, which for them was their own firsthand knowledge of the power of Yahweh over their pagan neighbors, and his ability to save and shape them as his people—despite their obscure origins, their lack of merit, and their disobedience. In the end, the Biblical writers concluded that Israel's election and survival were nothing less than a miracle. Who are we, their spiritual heirs, to disagree?

3

MONUMENTAL
ART AND
ARCHITECTURE
IN ANCIENT ISRAEL
IN THE PERIOD
OF THE
UNITED MONARCHY

THE United Monarchy in ancient Israel spans barely a century covering the reigns of the first three kings of Israel: Saul (ca. 1020–1000 B.C.), David (ca. 1000–960 B.C.), and Solomon (ca. 960–920 B.C.). The basic historical and chronological framework for the period is derived principally from the Hebrew Bible itself, especially the books of Samuel and 1 Kings, together with the more-or-less parallel account in Chronicles. These literary sources are manifestly closer to the events they purport to record, and therefore more reliable, than the Pentateuchal prehistory—though they do not, of course, by that virtue constitute modern historiography. We are dealing, rather, with "Deuteronomic history"—a composite, heavily editorialized work of a particular school of Israelite history writing, the objective of which may be called prophetic or theocratic history. From this account, however, we can abstract the main thread of a narrative concerning the chief public events that probably characterized the reigns of Saul, and particularly of David and Solomon.[1]

There are, nevertheless, several shortcomings in this outline. First is the obvious fact that the literary source materials, together with their interpretations, originated and were perpetuated in courtly and priestly circles, and were therefore establishment oriented. The focus is almost exclusively on public happenings, particularly large-scale political events, or on the deeds of prominent figures such as kings and prophets. Almost completely missing is the private history of other individuals; that is, we have little of such literary genres as biography, belles lettres, and other primary historical documents.

The second problem is one that pertains here. Is it possible to correlate the literary with the nonliterary remains that are becoming known, i.e., archaeological discoveries, so as to correct and supplement the bare historical outline previously available? This has been the general goal in the topographical and archaeological investigation of the Holy Land for more than a century. Indeed, the quest to reconstruct a historical background from external sources for written Biblical history has been partially successful with respect to several epochs. This is true especially for the period of the Judges and the later Divided Monarchy, where archaeology has supplied numerous, strikingly detailed data not recorded in the Bible, and moreover has provided corroboration for specific events that are mentioned. But it must be admitted that until very recently Palestinian and Biblical archaeology have been surprisingly silent regarding the United Monarchy, a period which not only was truly formative for ancient Israel but also witnessed the first flourishing of the material culture and the development of monumental art and architecture that should have left the clearest imprint on the archaeological record.

Sites, Distribution, Stratigraphy

Before we can appreciate the specific, individual archaeological discoveries that illumine this period, we must characterize the chief sites and their distribution, their state of excavation and publication, and some of the major stratigraphic problems confronted in the scholarly literature.

The pertinent archaeological sites and strata known to date are so few that virtually all can be schematized in a simple stratigraphic chart (table 4). I shall discuss them in geographical order, moving from north to south (figures 1, 15).

TABLE 4

Stratigraphic locations of archaeological sites from the periods of United Monarchy and Divided Monarchy

Sites	United Monarchy			Divided Monarchy
Palestine	Iron Ib (Israeli "Iron I")		Iron Ic (Israeli "Iron IIa")	Iron II ("IIb")
		Saul	David Solomon	Shishak
1100 B.C.		1000 B.C.		900 B.C.
Upper Galilee			Dan	→
(Aharoni)			gate	
Hazor	XI		xb-a ———————→	IX
ʿEn-gev			V IV	
Megiddo	VIb	VIa→ vb	va/ivb—→	IVa
Taʿanach			"cultic structure" →	
Tel ʿAmal		IV	III—→	
			Shiqmona "Town A"	
Tell Abu Hawam	(gap)	IVb	III ———————→	(gap)
Tell el-Farʿah N.	(gap)		IIIb ———————→	IIIa

TABLE 4 (continued)

Sites	United Monarchy				Divided Monarchy
Palestine	Iron Ib (Israeli "Iron I") — Saul — 1100 B.C.		Iron Ic (Israeli "Iron IIa") — David — Solomon — 1000 B.C.		Iron II ("IIb") — Shishak — 900 B.C.
Samaria			elements		I
Shechem	(gap)		XI		X
Gibeon			Upper pool city wall?		3
Beth-shemesh	III	(gap?)	IIa T.1,32,54 IIb		(gap)
Gibeah	"Building Period" II a-b	———————→		(gap?)	
Aphek				X	
Tel Qasile	XI	X		IX 2-1	
Gezer	XI	X	IX	VIII →	VII
Lachish	VI		V; T.116,218,223,521; Cave 6024		IV
Tell Beit Mirsim	B₂		B₃		A₁
Tel Sippor	II			(I)	
Tel Masos	II		I?		Arad
			(Malhata founded)? ←		XI
Beersheba	VIII		VII VI		V?
Ashdod	XII XI	X	IX		VIII
Tell Jemmeh	(levels 174-183 ———————————→ ?)				
Tell el-Hesi	(gap)		V		
			Negev forts ———→		(gap)
Tell el-Kheleifeh			I		II
Egypt	XXI Dynasty (ca. 1065-935 B.C.)		XXII Dynasty ——→ (ca. 935-735 B.C.)		
Syria	North="Dark Age" South=Rise of Aramaeans		"Neo-Hittites" ———→		
Mesopotamia	Babylonia=II Dyn. of Isin Assyria=Neo-Assyrian Empire ————————→				
Aegean	Crete=LM IIIC₂ Cyprus="Sub-Minoan"		"Early Proto-Geometric"		

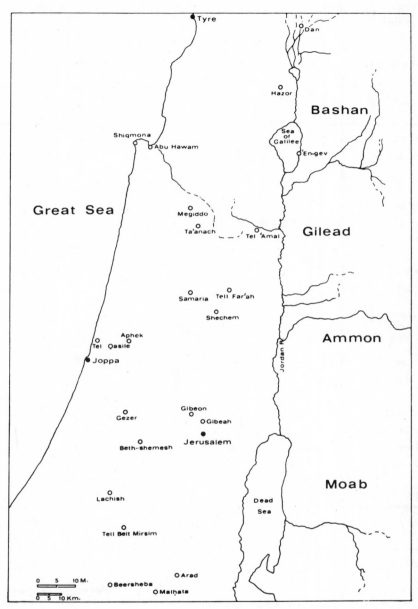

Figure 15. Map of the principal sites of the United Monarchy.

Galilee. In Galilee, especially Upper Galilee, surface survey has revealed many small twelfth- to eleventh-century Israelite settlements founded on virgin soil, but many of these apparently had been abandoned by the tenth century, and there has not yet been extensive excavation of the larger, centralized towns and cities that had developed to replace them.

Dan, later the northernmost boundary of Israel, is to be identified with the fifty-acre mound of Tell el-Qadi, on the Lebanese border. Partial excavations there (1966–85) brought to light on the south slopes a monumental three-entryway city gate and solid offsets-insets wall. The excavator, Avraham Biran, dated these constructions to the time of Jeroboam I, in the late tenth century B.C., but on the basis of supposed parallels with Megiddo and Beersheba other scholars have argued for a Davidic date. Only the gate plan has been published, but the preliminary reports suggest a date in the tenth or ninth century. Little can be attributed to the United Monarchy, which suggests that the site attained prominence only in the late tenth century B.C. and thereafter, when it became one of the royal sanctuaries of the Northern Kingdom under Jeroboam I.[2]

At the great 180-acre mound of Hazor, near the Huleh basin in Upper Galilee, excavated (1952–58) by Yadin and others, the Upper City is securely dated to the mid- to late tenth century B.C. Israelite settlement of the period was apparently restricted to a fortified citadel comprising approximately 6.5 acres, of which only a stretch of casemate wall and a fine four-entryway gate were exposed in Area A (see below and figure 16).[3]

At Megiddo in the Jezreel Valley, excavations by the University of Chicago (1925–39) partially cleared structures of the Davidic period, as well as a four-entryway city gate and a "palace" of Solomonic construction. Later soundings by Yadin (1960–67) dated the so-called "Solomonic stables" to the ninth century B.C.—thereby disqualifying them for consideration here. But the same soundings also revealed another large casemated residence and proved that beneath the misdated offsets-insets wall lay the true casemate (i.e. double) wall corresponding to the Solomonic gate (see below and figure 17).[4] Archaeological investigation thus confirmed that Megiddo was one of the most prominent Solomonic provincial administrative centers, as suggested by 1 Kings 9:15.

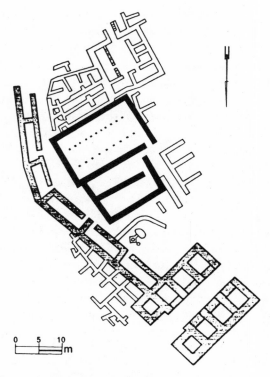

Figure 16. Plan of the Solomonic city gate and wall at Hazor (Str. x).
From Y. Yadin, *Hazor: The Rediscovery of a Great City of the Bible*, p. 195.

Excavation of a sister site in the Jezreel Valley, Ta'anach (1963–68),
revealed a "cultic structure" and a bizarre incense stand with an image
of Astarte, probably of the tenth century B.C. (see below).[5] But it would
appear that Ta'anach's history of occupation was complementary to that
of Megiddo, to the northwest, and it was largely deserted during the Solomonic heyday of its more powerful neighbor site.

Samaria. In Samaria the Israelite occupation was evidently much more
intensive since, as the German topographer Albrecht Alt argued long ago,

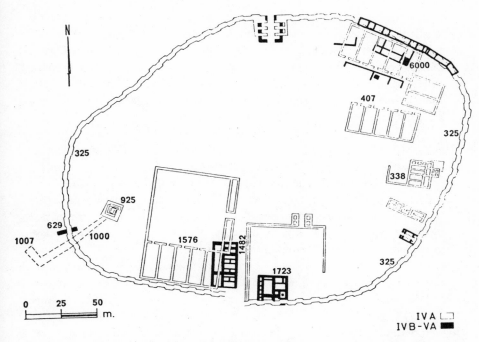

Figure 17. Plan of Megiddo in the Solomonic (Str. ivb–va) and Ahab periods (Str. iva). Note Solomonic "Palace 6000" and the stretch of casemate city wall to the north. From Y. Yadin, *Hazor: the Head of all These Kingdoms*, fig. 39.

the absence of Canaanite domination in the hill country gave ready access to the incoming tribes.

Tirzah, in the hills at the head of the ʿAin Farʿah, was excavated from 1946 to 1960. Though it was one of the earliest capitals of the Northern Kingdom in the ninth century, Tirzah in the tenth century B.C. had only a few courtyard houses of Israelite type and evidently was little more than a small town.[6]

Shechem, one of the principal Israelite centers of the pre-Monarchical period, was the focus of important American excavations led by G. E. Wright and others. However, the tenth century is represented only by some pottery and traces of a destruction, probably attributable to Pharaoh Shishak, ca. 918 B.C., and an Iron II rebuild of a casemate wall.[7]

Samaria, as is well known from both Biblical and archaeological sources, became the capital of the newly separated Northern Kingdom only in the ninth century B.C., under the Omrides, but the work of the Joint Expedition in the 1930s revealed a few sherds that indicate a possible pre-Omride settlement.[8]

Gibeon was excavated for six years (1956–62), but the only Israelite elements that appear to be earlier than Iron II are the upper water tunnel and possibly a re-use phase of an earlier city wall.[9]

Gibeah, on the northern outskirts of Jerusalem, was sounded by Albright (1922–23 and 1933), who declared a small tower-citadel (Fortress II) to be "Saul's rude fortress." The date was substantially confirmed by Paul Lapp's salvage campaign in 1964, which dated the casemate phase much later but affirmed the presence of the fort itself in "Building Period IIa–b," ca. 1025–950 B.C. The structure may indeed have been Saul's early palace, but alternatively it may have been a Philistine citadel (figure 18). In any case, its plan and contents, not yet fully published, feature little that is distinctly Israelite, much less of royal dimensions.[10]

Jerusalem, despite having been the Solomonic capital, has thus far revealed few traces of Iron Age remains *in situ* dating any earlier than the ninth century B.C. Scattered soundings carried out during the past century, and more systematic excavations by K. M. Kenyon, (1962–67), and several Israeli excavators, principally B. Mazar, N. Avigad, and Y. Shiloh since 1967, either have not yet reached these deep levels or, more likely, have failed to identify the fragmentary remains left by frequent destructions and continual rebuilding in later periods. There are, however, a few fine houses constructed on the eastern slopes of the City of David, probably of noble families attached to the court or Temple.[11] (The Temple will be discussed below.)

The Shephelah and Coastal Plain. The Israelites did not occupy the Shephelah and coastal plain until the Davidic-Solomonic period, and even then did not effectively control the area. Beth-shemesh, a dominant site in the buffer zone near the mouth of the Vale of Elah, was excavated be-

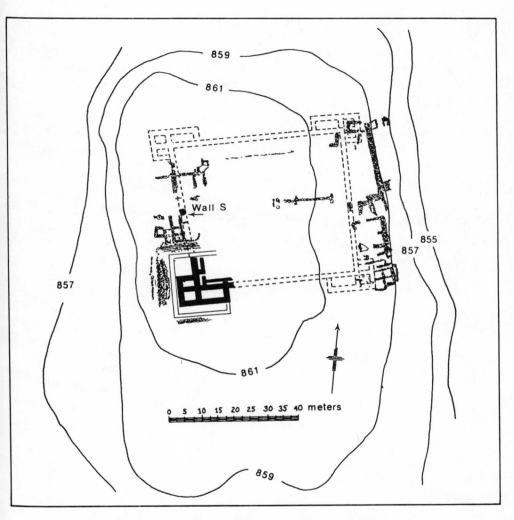

Figure 18. Plan of "Fortress II" at Gibeah (tenth century B.C.).

tween 1928 and 1933. Despite faulty stratigraphy, it has been shown that
Stratum IIa is probably Davidic and IIb Solomonic. The principal elements indicating the establishment of an Israelite settlement on this erst-
while Philistine site are an early casemate city wall, a large residency,
and a typical four-room structure of the Israelite type that is possibly a
granary.

Gezer, guarding the entrance to the Ajalon Valley at the juncture of
the Coastal Plain and the northern Shephelah, was excavated early in this
century (1902–9) by R. A. S. Macalister. However, only modern excava-

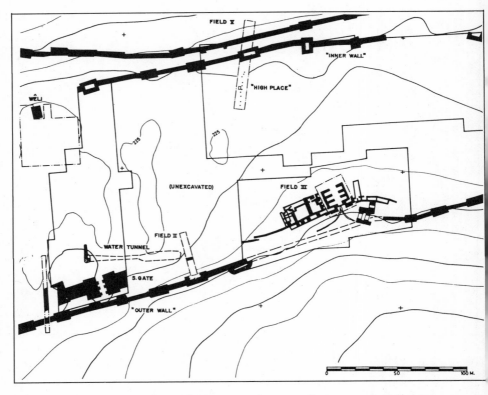

Figure 19. Plan of part of the excavated areas at Gezer; note the Solomonic
city gate, casemate wall, and "palace" in Field III. From W. G. Dever
et al., *Gezer* II, plate 1.

tions (W. G. Dever, H. D. Lance, and others, 1964–74) clarified and correctly dated the splendid four-entryway city gate and casemate wall of Field III to the Solomonic period. (On Macalister's "Maccabean Castle," see below and figure 19). It is now known that a casemate building west of the gate is a tenth-century "palace" comparable to those of Solomonic Megiddo (below). Elsewhere there are traces of tenth-century domestic structures, but it appears that Gezer was little more than an Israelite outpost after the Egyptian destruction and the Solomonic takeover. [12]

Judea. Intensive surface surveys in recent years have demonstrated that the hill country south of Jerusalem was densely settled by the Israelites, beginning in the ninth or eighth century and culminating in the seventh century B.C. However, the tenth century, still poorly represented, may have seen relatively spare occupation.

Lachish, the principal fortress in the southern Judean hills, revealed few clear tenth-century remains except for a few tombs found during the British excavation of Starkey (1935–38). But Israeli excavations led by the Israeli archaeologist David Ussishkin since 1973 suggest that the monumental four-entryway Iron II gate of Strata IV–III may have been established as early as Stratum V of the tenth century B.C., and also proved that the monumental "Palace A" belongs to Stratum V. The four-room house excavated earlier has also been considered tenth century. Finally, Aharoni's excavations (1966–68) suggest that a small cult room beneath the "Solar Shrine" should be attributed to Stratum V (more on this below; see figure 20). [13]

Tell Beit Mirsim (Albright's Debir or Kiryat-sefer) still provides what is perhaps the clearest evidence of Solomonic constructions in the south, in the casemate wall uncovered in the 1926–32 excavations.

The Negev. Until recently it was believed that the Negev had at no time been more than sparsely populated, least of all under Israelite occupation. However, recent Israeli exploration and several major excavations have revealed an extensive Israelite presence, broadening the picture.

Iron Age Beersheba, east of the modern town, is a small (three-acre) but impressive citadel, almost entirely cleared by Aharoni in the 1969–75

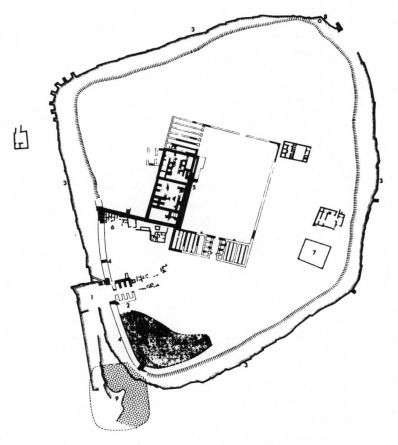

Figure 20. Plan of excavated areas at Lachish; note the city gate (2), "Palace A" (5); the "Solar Shrine" is seen to the extreme right (above). From D. Ussishkin et al., *Tel Aviv* 10, fig. 2.

excavations. Its major phase is eighth and seventh century B.C. Stratum VI, however, with its four-room house, is probably late tenth century, and Stratum V, with its glacis or rampart, solid offsets/insets wall, and triple-entryway gate, has been attributed to the tenth century by the excavator but is more likely late ninth century in date.[14]

To the east, Arad poses similar problems, although Aharoni's 1962–67 excavations of the Iron Age acropolis suggests that the earliest casemated fort and possibly the temple-sanctuary (discussed below) date to the tenth century.[15]

Related to the Beersheba-Arad complex are two other sites, both only partially investigated in connection with Aharoni's Tel Aviv project in the Negev. Soundings at Tel Malhata (1967–71) have bared a solid town wall and a public building of the tenth century B.C. At nearby Tell Masos (Biblical Hormah?) there have been revealed several fine four-room houses of the Israelite style of the eleventh century, continuing into the early tenth century B.C. (see chapter 2).

Surveys and soundings in the Negev farther south, principally of Y. Aharoni and R. Cohen in the past decade, have placed on our map a string of more than forty small Israelite forts, many of them apparently dating only to the tenth century B.C.[16] These forts seem to have been intended to guard Judah's southern and eastern borders during the Monarchy.

Two sites founded in the tenth century B.C., but continuing in use throughout Iron II, represent the maximum Israelite expansion in the desert. Tell el-Kheleifeh, Solomon's seaport on the Red Sea near modern Elat-Aqaba, was excavated by Nelson Glueck (1937–40). The date of the founding of the fortress and casemate enclosure of Stratum I (never fully published) has been widely debated but probably is tenth century B.C. However, Glueck's much publicized "Solomon's smelter" must be given up, since more recent study of the material has ruled out any connection with copper working.[17]

The Israelite pilgrim site and fortress at Kadesh-barnea in eastern Sinai was investigated in 1956 and has been excavated further since 1978. Building Period I, the founding level, has barely been reached but lies below the ninth–eighth century phase II building and is tenth century in date. (Quite surprising is the complete absence of any pre–tenth century material, leaving Kadesh-barnea of the "Wilderness tradition" without any evidence whatsoever.[18])

This summary of known tenth-century sites and their distribution is based on less systematic and thorough excavation than would be desirable. Nevertheless, the emergent picture of the Israelite occupation of Canaan is probably accurate in broad outline. It reveals that the twelfth- to eleventh-century settlements of the period of the Judges were restricted by Canaanite and Philistine opposition to Upper Galilee, the hill country, parts of the Shephelah, and the northern Negev. For this pattern, particularly important is the new evidence of Aharoni's surveys in Galilee, and especially the discovery of small early Israelite sites at ʿAi and Kh. Raddana near Jerusalem, at ʿIzbet Ṣarṭeh near Aphek, and at Tel Masos near Beersheba. These early Israelite settlements, many of which came to an end by the late eleventh century B.C., tend to confirm the view of Alt and Noth on the non-military aspects of the Israelite occupation of Canaan (see above, chapter 2). Then, in the tenth century B.C., particularly under Solomon, there was a marked tendency toward centralization and urban development, with an accompanying increase in population, a rise in prosperity, and the development of monumental art and architecture, all reflected in the archaeological record.

Town Planning and Domestic Buildings

Having surveyed the general early Israelite settlement pattern, the major tenth-century sites, and the material safely attributable to the United Monarchy, we now turn to more detailed treatment of specific categories.

No direct archaeological evidence yet exists for centralized town planning—at least of domestic quarters—in the towns that we presume were rapidly built up or first founded in the early Monarchy. This may be the case simply because to date there has been no large-scale clearance of any tenth-century site. Tirzah, although the exposure was small, did produce evidence of differences between groups of "rich" and "poor" houses in *Niveau* III, which could be interpreted in terms of social stratification, if not of town planning.

Elsewhere, the only Iron Age towns cleared sufficiently to present an overall picture have given us, quite naturally, the plan of the uppermost levels, which have not then been removed. The best recent example is the well laid out eighth- to seventh-century town of Beersheba III–II (figure 21). The older plans of seventh-century Tell Beit Mirsim or of ninth- to eighth-century Tell en-Naṣbeh (Mizpah) are also instructive. However, the striking homogeneity of tenth-century fortifications and their long, continuous rebuild on the same architectural plan have been noted by many and have been taken as evidence for centralized town planning from the earliest stages. If this is true, then in the case of domestic architecture as well, we may reasonably extrapolate from the later town plan of those sites first founded in the tenth century, such as Beersheba,

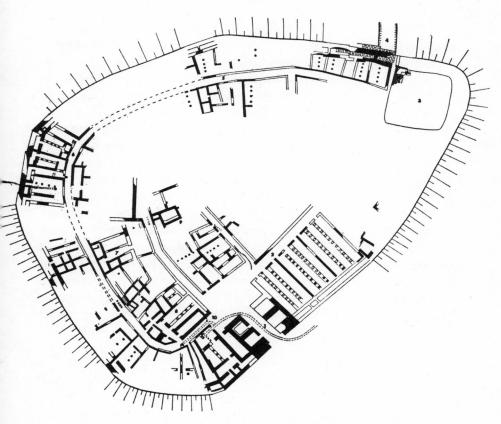

Figure 21. Plan of the excavated areas at Beersheba, Str. III–II (eighth-seventh century B.C.). From Y. Aharoni, *Tel Aviv* 1, fig. 1.

for the original layout. Particularly in the case of royal provincial administrative centers, we should expect to see evidence for crown supervision, and indeed Megiddo va–ivb, though only partially cleared, gives us such evidence in the layout of the city defenses and the two "palaces" (see below). It is doubtful, however, that smaller towns, or villages of lesser importance, were similarly laid out or were planned according to standardized specifications. As villages and hamlets of early Iron i grew rapidly into sizeable towns, or new settlements were planted on virgin soil due to population growth and increasing prosperity, urban development was probably difficult to control and quite haphazard.

We may not yet be able to see the overall picture of tenth-century town planning, but the development of a standardized plan for individual structures that served many purposes is clear. I refer to the well-known four-room building, which has a long history but is first encountered in the twelfth and eleventh centuries, and then more frequently in such tenth-century sites as Beth-shemesh, Lachish, Tell Qasile, and Tell el-Ḥesi, among others. This stereotyped building plan, in which a long back room and two side rooms surround a central court (sometimes unroofed), seems to have been adapted for private dwellings (figure 22), for larger public structures of various sorts, for granaries, and possibly for other uses. The late Yigal Shiloh surveyed the available evidence and concluded that the four-room building is an eleventh- or tenth-century Israelite innovation.[19] On the other hand, there is some evidence from two large twelfth-century houses at Gezer that the Philistines or "Sea Peoples" may have introduced the idea from the Mediterranean sphere. However, at present we cannot point conclusively to either an Aegean or to a local Canaanite background for this distinctive style of Iron Age courtyard house, so its development may stem from an indigenous style of early Iron Age peasant farmhouse.

Defense Works

With regard to fortifications, we have somewhat more data, due in part to the monumental character and excellent construction of town walls and gates, which tended to survive even repeated destruction, to be rebuilt

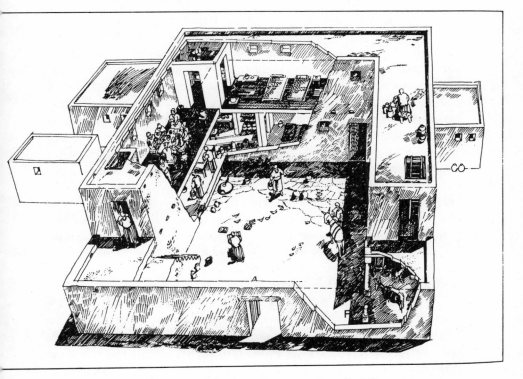

Figure 22. Reconstruction of a typical Iron Age or "Israelite" four-room courtyard house (Shechem, eighth century B.C.). From *Great People of the Bible and
How They Lived* (Pleasantville, New York: Readers Digest Assoc., 1974), p. 140.

and reused for many centuries, and to leave substantial remains extant
today. Also, the orientation of much Biblical archaeology to political history has meant that most excavations at Israelite sites have concentrated
on tracing the development and destruction of fortifications, often to the
neglect of the domestic quarters (see above, chapter 1).

We have already noted the casemate chambered city walls that first appear at tenth-century Israelite sites. We have firmly dated Solomonic casemates in Hazor x, Megiddo-va–ivb, Gezer viii, Tell Beit Mirsim B$_3$,

Beth-shemesh IIa (possibly Davidic), and Tell Qasile X; and we may add with less certainty the tenth-century casemates from Shiqmona, Arad XI, Tell el-Kheleifeh I, and the several Negev forts. These distinctive double, partitioned walls were long thought to be of Syrian or Anatolian origin, but recently discovered Middle Bronze II examples from Hazor, Taᶜanach, and Shechem demonstrate that there was a local Canaanite tradition of casemate construction that goes back at least to the seventeenth century B.C. The thickness of the tenth-century Israelite casemates averages one-and-a-half to two meters in width for each wall, and in peacetime the chambers served for storage or even living quarters, as examples at many sites attest. The earliest Israelite casemates were built mostly during the Solomonic period, and indeed, with the possible exception of a solid offsets-insets wall at Beersheba V, these distinctive walls characterize that period almost exclusively. In Iron II, during the ninth to seventh centuries B.C., these casemates were replaced at many sites with solid walls, but nevertheless they continued to be re-used and even constructed right to the end of the Israelite Monarchy.

City gates brought to light by excavations are fewer. Apart from the disputed three-entryway gates at Dan and Beersheba, (which, despite Aharoni, are basically ninth century B.C.), the typical tenth-century gate is of the four-entryway type, attested thus far by striking coincidence at three of the four sites listed in I Kings 9:15–17 as having been fortified by Solomon: Hazor, Megiddo, and Gezer. Only Jerusalem, mostly unexcavated at tenth-century levels, is missing. The only other four-entryway gates excavated to date are the massive four-entryway gate of Lachish IV–II (the groundplan of which, when clarified, may go back to Stratum V of the tenth century), and the equally massive gate of Stratum IX in Area M at Ashdod, which may be eleventh century in date and possibly suggests a Philistine origin for these so-called Solomonic city gates (figure 23).

The story of the discovery of the nearly identical Solomonic city gates at Hazor, Megiddo, and Gezer is well known. R. A. S. Macalister had cleared the western half of the Gezer gate in 1902–9 excavations but had termed it a "Maccabean Castle," mistakenly supposing it to be part of the citadel of Simon Maccabeus and dating it to the second century B.C.

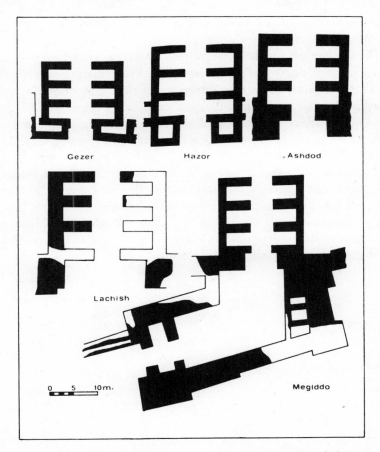

Figure 23. Plan of the known four-entryway city gates, all probably tenth century B.C. From Z. Herzog, *The City-gate in Eretz-Israel*, figs. 80–84.

Thus the Gezer gate went unnoticed for decades. In the 1920s and 1930s, however, the University of Chicago excavators at Megiddo brought to light the first recognizable and datable example of such a city gate in Stratum va/IVb. The complex includes the inner four-entryway (three-chamber) gate of fine ashlar (or dressed) masonry, an outer ramp with a lower two-entryway gate-tower, and, as Yadin later demonstrated, a connected casemate wall.

Then following his own excavations at Hazor (1955–58), where a nearly identical inner gate and casemate wall were discovered in Stratum x on the Acropolis, Yadin again turned to the plan of Macalister's "Maccabean Castle" and made the brilliant suggestion that here was a hitherto unrecognized Solomonic city gate of similar type. He cited the text of I Kings 9:15–17, and further suggested that all three gates "were in fact built by Solomon's architects from identical blueprints."

The subsequent excavations at Gezer, led by myself and others (in 1964–67), completed the excavation of the buried Gezer gate (Stratum VIII) and dated it on ceramic evidence to the tenth century B.C., dramatically confirming both Yadin's intuition and the Biblical record (figures 19, 23). The dimensions of the Gezer Gate are even closer to the dimensions of the other two than Yadin surmised:

TABLE 5
Comparative dimensions of three tenth-century B.C. city gates

	Megiddo	Hazor	Gezer
Length	20.3	20.3	19.0
Width	17.5	18.0	16.2
Between towers	6.5	6.1	5.5
Entrance width	4.2	4.2	4.1
Wall width	1.6	1.6	1.6
Total casemate width	(approx. 5.5)	5.4	5.4

Like the Megiddo gate, the one at Gezer features fine ashlar construction, has an outer ramp and offset two-entryway gate-tower, exhibits hinges and bolt holes of double doors inside the threshold, and has a large drain running through the gate passageway. Moreover, like both the Megiddo and Hazor gates, it is connected to a casemate wall.[20] Thus, the parallels between the three Solomonic gates alluded to in I Kings 9 and those brought to light by excavation are so close that we must posit royal supervision in the construction of fortified, provincial administrative centers in the tenth century B.C. Here is a rare, dramatic instance of archaeology turning up actual structures mentioned specifically in the Bible.

Other "Royal" Constructions

We turn now to a consideration of other categories of royal architecture. In addition to the defense works discussed above, we possess some knowledge of other buildings at the regional administrative centers which Biblical scholars have reconstructed from the Solomonic province lists in 1 Kings 4:7–19.

Megiddo provides our most complete data (see figure 17). From the Chicago excavations we have several structures, notably Building 1482 and particularly Building 1723, probably the governor's palace. The latter is at the south of the mound just inside the city wall, a splendidly constructed building of ashlar and rubble-filled masonry similar to that of the Stratum va–ivb Solomonic gate. The enclosed compound, with its own triple-entryway gate, measures some sixty meters square; the main structure is twenty meters by twenty-two meters and has a dozen rooms surrounding a central court, as well as a tower staircase indicating a second floor (figure 24). This palatial structure has properly been compared

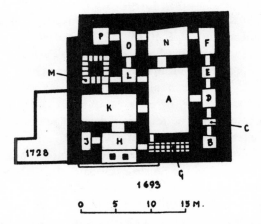

Figure 24. Building 1723 at Megiddo, the southern Solomonic "palace"; note the central court (A) and the staircase (M). From D. Ussishkin, *IEJ* 16, fig. 4.

with the Assyrian-style *bīt ḫilâni* familiar from contemporary sites to the north—especially at Zinjirli (ancient Samᶜal in North Syria), where the ninth-eighth century Hilani III and "Palaces J–K" of Kings Kilamua and Bar-Rakkib are extremely close (figure 25). Comparable examples also come from Sakçegözu and Karatepe in Anatolia, Tell Tayinat in Syria, and Tell Halaf (ancient Gozan) in Mesopotamia. It seems likely that this southern structure is, in fact, the palace of Solomon's governor, Baᶜana, son of Ahilud, mentioned in 1 Kings 4:12.

In his campaigns of 1960 to 1967, Yadin uncovered another, even larger palatial structure along the north casemate wall, in area BB just east of the gate, also attributable to Stratum va–ivb. "Palace 6000" was twenty-one by twenty-eight meters, built of fine ashlar masonry laid in header-stretcher fashion with field stones in the in-between stretches, like the southern "palace." The arrangement of its eight rooms around a central court also strongly suggests the North Syrian–Anatolian *bīt ḫilâni*.

The existence of close northern parallels for both the Megiddo palaces only reinforces the unanimous Biblical witness that Solomon, having no native Israelite tradition in art and architecture to draw on, employed artisans and architects from Phoenicia. If we may assume that the southern, enclosed Palace 1723 was the district governor's residence, then the northern Palace 6000, like many of the other known *bīt ḫilâni*s, was probably used as a reception court and for other ceremonial functions (perhaps even as a guest residence for the King).[21]

Another structure that has been compared to Palace 6000 at Megiddo is a large building shown on Macalister's plans at Gezer, adjoining what we now know to be a Solomonic city gate (cf. figure 19, above). However, the final season of the current excavations in 1984 showed that while the original phase of this building is indeed Solomonic in date, it is not a *bīt ḫilâni* or even necessarily part of a palace. It is, rather, a large, exceptionally well-built barracks or guardroom complex near the gate, destroyed with the gate in the Shishak campaign ca. 918 B.C.[22]

Finally, the "Residency" at Lachish has been shown by the latest excavations to have been founded in its first phase (Palace A) late in Stratum V, and is thus either late tenth or early ninth century B.C. in date. It is also a *ḫilâni*-type structure roughly thirty-two meters square (cf. figure 20).

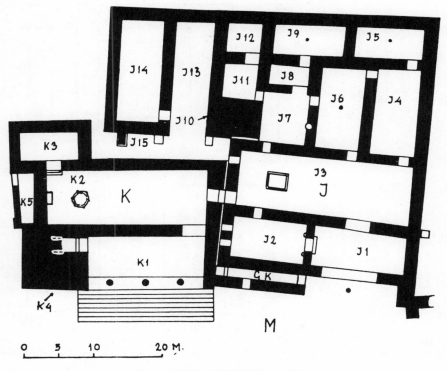

Figure 25. "Palaces J–K" at Zinjirli (ca. ninth century B.C.).
From D. Ussishkin, *IEJ* 16, fig. 1.

The last category of "royal constructions" I shall discuss—the so-called stables or storehouses—may be treated briefly. The latest excavation and research have shown that most of these colonnaded structures are post-tenth-century B.C., including the famous "Solomonic stables" at Megiddo attributed to Stratum VIa/IVb, which Yadin has shown belong rather to IVa of the period of Ahab. The only examples that may be dated to the tenth century B.C. are those at Tell Abu Hawan IVb, Tell Qasile IX, and possibly Tell el-Ḥesi V (figure 26). These buildings, particularly the ones at Megiddo, have often been interpreted as stables, but current theory regards them as public storehouses, perhaps part of the construction of regional administrative centers under crown supervision.

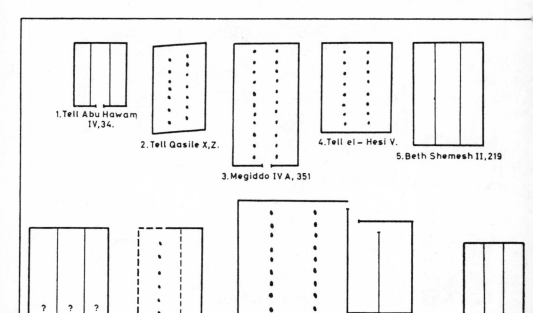

1. Tell Abu Hawam IV,34.

2. Tell Qasile X,Z.

3. Megiddo IV A, 351

4. Tell el – Hesi V.

5. Beth Shemesh II,219

6. Lachish IV,1031   7. Lachish III–II,1003

8. Hazor VIII–VII,71+69

9. Arad VIII

Figure 26. Schematic plans of typical tripartite buildings of the Iron Age, either stables or storehouses. From Y. Shiloh, *IEJ* 20, fig. 2.

Cultic Structures

By far the best known religious edifice of the tenth century B.C. is the famous Temple of Solomon. The design and construction of this splendid temple are elaborated in considerable detail in 1 Kings 6–8 (and reflected also in Ezekiel's vision of the restored Temple in Ezekiel 40–47). Thus far, however, not a single trace of such a temple has come to light from excavations anywhere in Jerusalem. The lack of extant remains is undoubtedly due to the complete destruction of the Solomonic Temple by the Babylonians, as well as the destruction of the later Persian Temple on the same spot, the thorough clearance to bedrock by the Roman engineers who erected the Second Temple on the site, and finally the construction of the Dome of the Rock by the Caliph Abd el-Malik in 691 A.D. In any case, Islamic sentiment, Orthodox Jewish tradition, and international law combine to render any systematic archaeological investigation of the Temple Mount out of the question.

Even in the absence of direct archaeological confirmation, we have a surprising wealth of detailed comparative data to aid in elucidating the Biblical texts and in reconstructing the Temple of Solomon.[23] First of all, the tripartite ground plan of the Biblical description of the Solomonic Temple features three rooms arranged along a central axis: the outer *ulam* or vestibule, the central *hekhal* or court, and the innermost *devir* or "Holy of Holies" (figure 27). Until a few years ago no examples of such tripartite temples were known outside of the Biblical description, but in the 1930s

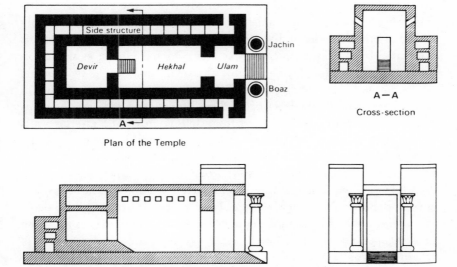

Figure 27. Schematic plan and section of the Solomonic Temple in Jerusalem. From *Interpreter's Dictionary of the Bible*, Vol. 4, p. 537.

the University of Chicago excavations at Tell Tayinat in Syria turned up a ninth-century temple which closely fitted the Biblical description and thus confirmed the Phoenician provenance of the basic temple design, in accordance with 1 Kings 5:8ff. Then in Yadin's 1955–58 excavations at Hazor, a local Canaanite temple of similar plan was brought to light in Area H, dating to the Late Bronze Age (ca. fifteenth–fourteenth centuries B.C.). Finally, in 1973, I reinvestigated part of the old so-called Middle Bronze Age palace near the Northwest Gate at Shechem and discerned the plan of a tripartite temple of the seventeenth and sixteenth centuries B.C., the earliest such temple yet found in Palestine. Mention should also be made of the Middle Bronze Age Temple in Area D of Tell Mardikh (ancient Ebla) in Syria. Thus it is clear that the basic ground plan of Solomon's temple in Jerusalem was simply borrowed from a local Syro-Palestinian or Canaanite temple style that dated back nearly a thousand years.

Second, the superstructure and decoration of the Solomonic Temple are illuminated by several archaeological discoveries of the period. The distinctive, Phoenician-style "ashlar" (or finely dressed) masonry, probably laid in alternate header and stretcher fashion (1 Kings 5:17, 7:9–12), is illustrated by the Solomonic gates at Megiddo and Hazor, as well as in the ninth-century Tell Tayinat temple already discussed. The twin pillars of "Jachin and Boaz" at the entrance (1 Kings 7:15–22) are reflected in many Syro-Anatolian temples of the Late Bronze Age and Iron Age, including the example already cited from Tell Tayinat. The interior walls of the Temple were paneled in cedar wood from Lebanon (1 Kings 6:15–18); this suggests lower stone orthostats or dados, with upper wooden panels affixed by mortise-and-tenon, a typically Syrian style of decoration known from the Late Bronze Area H temple at Hazor, as well as from the later Tell Tayinat temple. Finally, the carved and gilded decoration of the woodwork and the entrance columns is described as featuring gourds, open flowers, lilies, palm trees, pomegranates, and networks of "chain" designs (1 Kings 6:18, 29, 15–22). These motifs are well illustrated by the nearly contemporary ninth- and eighth-century Phoenician and Israelite ivory carved panels from Nimrud, Arslan-Tash, Samaria, Hazor, and elsewhere—especially the palm or "palmette" design, which appears not only on the ivories, but on many seals (see below). This design was ultimately schematized in the Proto-Aeolic (or Proto-Ionic) capitals, of which more than thirty are now known from Israelite sites of the tenth through eighth centuries B.C. (figure 28).

Third, the interior furnishing of the Solomonic Temple may be illustrated from archaeological finds, especially the two-winged cherubim of the "Holy of Holies" (1 Kings 6:23–28), which are now illustrated in numerous ninth–eighth century ivories and in several Iron Age seal impressions (figure 29). The particular expression of the cherub in the art and iconography of Israel is clearly less Assyrian and more Phoenician, combining as it does the characteristically mixed, even bungled motifs of both Mesopotamian and Egyptian art. Thus, once again the Phoenician

Figure 28. Examples of the "palmette" or "Proto-Aeolic" capitals (tenth-eighth century B.C.). From Y. Shiloh, *The Proto-Aeolic Capital and Israelite Ashlar Masonry*, fig. 11.

Figure 29. Carved ivory inlay from Samaria, with Phoenician-style cherub and "sacred tree" (ninth-eighth century B.C.). From J. W. Crowfoot, J. M. Crowfood, and K. M. Kenyon, *Samaria-Sebaste* II, plate 5:3a.

prototypes of the Solomonic Temple, as stated specifically in the Bible, are confirmed by comparative material provided by archaeology.

Fourth, the forecourt of the Temple in Jerusalem may be better understood in the light of such recent discoveries as the large "horned altar" from eighth-century Beersheba, which recalls the great altar of burnt offerings in Ezekiel 43:13–17. The ten-wheeled bronze stands and the ten bronze lavers of the Temple forecourt described in 1 Kings are also seen in examples from earlier Phoenician art, including several which have precisely the pomegranate decoration mentioned in the Bible. Finally, the "pots, shovels, and basins" (1 Kings 7:40, 45), which were probably used for incense and burnt offerings, have several parallels in archaeological finds of the period, as for instance at Dan.

Fifth, several structures related to the Solomonic Temple are mentioned in 1 Kings: the "Millo," the "House of the Forest of Lebanon," the "Hall of Pillars," a harem for wives and concubines, and a separate residence for Solomon's own royal residence. As stated above, few actual traces of these buildings have been found or are likely to be found. But it has been persuasively argued that these several structures formed a unified complex of the type attested in the North Syrian–Anatolian *bīt ḫilâni*, examples of which we have already noted as parallels for the regional palaces at Solomonic Megiddo. The basic plan of the tenth-century Acropolis in Jerusalem is undoubtedly seen in the ninth- and eighth-century complexes at Tell Halaf (ancient Gozan) in Mesopotamia, at Karatepe and Sakçegözu in Anatolia, and at Tell Tayinat in Syria. But the most complete example is Hilâni III and Palaces J–K at Zinjirli, ancient Samʿal, the capital of the kings of Kilamua and Bar-Rakkib (cf. figure 25, above). Here we see all the elements of Solomon's "Royal Quarter" in Jerusalem. We can even illustrate details of the individual buildings and their furnishings with findings from archaeology: the ashlar masonry (1 Kings 7:9–10), the alternating stone and wood courses and the cedar paneling (1 Kings 7:11–12), the throne borne on the wings of lion-cherubim (cf. 1 Kings 6:23–28), and the portable braziers.

One especially elusive reference noted above—to Solomon's "Millo" (1 Kings 9:15, 24)—now seems to have been illuminated by archaeology. The Hebrew word means a fill of some sort, but the references do not

make clear what this was or how it related to Solomon's other constructions. Recently, however, Yigal Shiloh re-cleared and correctly dated for
the first time an elaborate stepped stone platform south of the Temple
Mount. It is Solomonic in date and seems almost certainly to be the
"Millo," that is, an artificial terrace, both to consolidate Jerusalem's steep
slopes at this point, and to provide a podium for the various new public
and domestic buildings to be built there (figure 30).[24]

In addition to the Solomonic Temple—which was, of course, the focus
of Solomon's attempt to centralize religion in Jerusalem and as such the
only national shine—we have some archaeological evidence of local Israelite sanctuaries of the tenth century B.C.

At Megiddo, the Chicago excavators found in the courtyard of Building
2081 of Stratum VA a small "cult corner" which contained among other
items two small "horned" limestone altars, chalices, and cultic stands of
stone and terra cotta. A similar household shrine was found in 1968 by
Aharoni below the Persian-Hellenistic "Solar Shrine" at Lachish, "Cult
Room 49," dating to Stratum V of the tenth century. The finds were
strikingly similar to those at Megiddo: on benches around the small room
were a horned limestone altar, four ceramic incense stands, seven chalices,
and other miscellaneous pottery. Finally, Lapp found in tenth-century
levels at Taʿanach a "cultic installation" featuring a stone slab–lined basin
with two stelae or *maṣṣēbôth*; nearby were more than a hundred pig
astragali, a stone mold for casting Astarte figurines, and a fantastic cult
stand similar to one the German excavators had found sixty years earlier
(see chapter 4).

Two larger cultic installations of the tenth century B.C. have been interpreted as actual full-scale temples, though in both cases are more wisely
regarded merely as local sanctuaries, no doubt Israelite if not truly "Yahwistic." The first is in Stratum XI of the Upper City at Arad, the basal
level, where Aharoni uncovered a sanctuary of several rooms around a central courtyard with a large fieldstone altar. At the western end was a cella
featuring two small limestone altars flanking the stepped entrance; nearby
was a well-dressed stela or *maṣṣēbāh* (figure 31). Earlier, Aharoni had
compared the plan of the Arad structure with the Jerusalem Temple, and
he later turned to the wilderness Tabernacle for a parallel. But the Arad

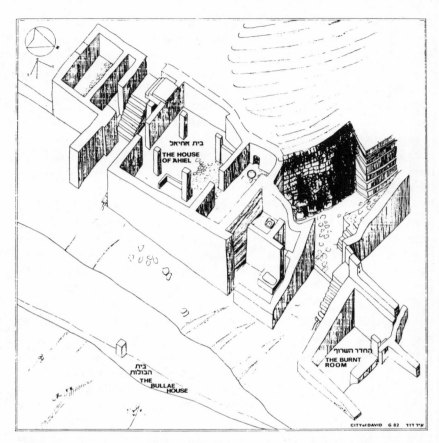

Figure 30. Cut-away plan of tenth-century B.C. "House of Aḥiel," built atop the stepped-stone platform or "Millo" in Jerusalem. From Y. Shiloh, *Excavations at the City of David I. 1978–1982*, fig. 25.

sanctuary need not be understood in such grandiose terms. Furthermore, the contents and the related pottery have not been published, and the stratigraphy of Stratum XI has been much debated, leaving both date and function of the Arad cult installation in doubt.

The rather poor Stratum IX rebuild of the tenth-century Philistine

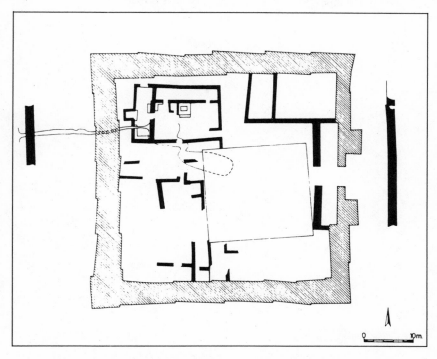

Figure 31. Plan of the Arad temple of Str. XI (tenth century B.C.).
From Y. Aharoni, *BA* 31, fig. 12.

temple of Tel Qasile X has been attributed by the excavator to the Israelite
conquerors and settlers, but it is not at all clear that the building continued to serve as a cult center at this stage of history.

With this survey of the building remains of the Davidic-Solomonic era,
we come to the end of our treatment of the architecture of the period.
It must be stressed that these remains are not only the earliest evidence
we possess of monumental architecture in ancient Israel, but they are
among the most impressive. We can now understand the biblical tradition
of 1 Kings 10:4–5, which relates of the visit of the Queen of Sheba to
view Solomon's splendid buildings in Jerusalem that she was so astonished
that "there was no more spirit left in her."

4

ARCHAEOLOGY
RECONSTRUCTS
THE LOST BACKGROUND
OF THE
ISRAELITE CULT

M OST studies of the archaeological and historical background of early Israelite religion have suffered from two fundamental deficiencies. First, they have analyzed the two classes of pertinent data—textual and artifactual—in isolation from each other. Moreover, the exclusion or mis-application of the archaeological evidence and the overinterpretation of the literary evidence have produced a distorted picture. Thus we have many "Old Testament theologies" but no comprehensive "history of the religion of ancient Israel" that takes advantage of the potential of modern interdisciplinary inquiry—textual and theological studies coupled with archaeology, ethnology, and comparative religion. Second, previous stud-ies have stressed the "uniqueness" of Israelite religion to the neglect of those features it shared with ancient oriental religions in general, and with Late Bronze Age Canaanite religion in particular. The resulting re-constructions have been arbitrary and ultimately unpersuasive.

I will here seek to redress the balance by giving precedence to the con-tribution of archaeology—conceived as a newer and independent, yet in-terrelated, discipline with unique explanatory potential—and by adopt-ing a phenomenological or "functionalist" approach to the study of religion, relying more on sociological and anthropological models than on theological method, and more on material remains of the cult than on ideology.[1]

The specific questions I shall address, using the methodology outlined above, are the following: What was the actual nature of early Israelite religious practice? What was the social milieu in Late Bronze-Iron I Pales-tine in which it flourished? What were the specific factors in continuity with the Canaanite cultural sphere that may have played a formative role in shaping the early Israelite cult? And finally, what was distinctively "Is-raelite" in this religion?

The particular approach and methodology adopted here require the clearest possible definition of the terms to be used hereafter. First, for the purpose of the following discussion, I shall define *religion* as a set of symbolic thought forms and acts that relate human beings to the ultimate conditions of their existence, perceived as the Holy. Second, and conse-quently, religion will be considered here in two aspects. Its aspect of thought, or *theology*, will be defined as the intellectual and moral systematization of religious belief. Its second aspect, and the primary concern of this discussion, is *cult*, or the individual and communal acting out of religious beliefs in worship and ritual—that is, the *practice* of religion. Archaeology, the remaining significant referent of this discussion, will continue to be defined as simply the science of material culture.

General Problems and Methodologies in the Reconstruction of Israelite Religion

We shall begin with the limitations of the textual evidence. What we have known until recently about Israelite religion (like Israelite history) comes almost exclusively from the Hebrew Bible, which preserves our only roughly contemporary literary data. To be sure, the rich corpus of fourteenth- to thirteenth-century B.C. cuneiform texts found in the 1920s and 1930s at ancient Ugarit on the coast of Syria has given us a fascinating glimpse into the heretofore mysterious and exotic world of Canaanite religion in the centuries immediately preceding Israel's emergence. More recently, archaeology has brought to light texts that illuminate the religions of Israel's neighbors, such as the Aramaeans, Phoenicians, Ammonites, Moabites, and Edomites.[2] But for Israel proper, the Bible itself has remained almost our sole textual witness. And the Hebrew Bible, despite its abundance of descriptions of Israelite belief and practice—indeed, its seeming preoccupation with religion—is severely limited as a historical source for several reasons.

First, the Biblical texts in their present form are often later—sometimes centuries later—than the events they purport to describe. For instance, the priestly legislation in Leviticus describing the sacrificial system appears to be set in the Mosaic period, but modern scholarship has shown that the literary form is archaizing and that in fact the book derives mostly from the post-Exilic period (nearly a millennium later), when the returnees from Babylon were attempting to restore their national identity by reinstituting earlier temple practices. If this is the *Sitz im Leben*, or cultural setting, then Leviticus, even though it contains some older material, may tell us very little about conditions during the period of the

Judges or the Monarchy, much less the Mosaic era. Even the genuinely historical elements contained in Joshua, Judges, and Samuel-Kings, in their present form, mostly date no further back than the tenth or ninth century B.C., and the final redaction is from the seventh to fourth centuries.

Second, the Biblical texts, in part because of their lateness, present an idealized scheme of religion that has somewhat arbitrarily harmonized several differing elements in the picture. For instance, we know that there never was a single monolithic religion of all Israel. Rather, there existed, often side by side, various strands, such as the partly Canaanite cult of the period of the Judges; the "official" religion of the Jerusalem temple and the royal cultus in the Monarchy; a "popular" religion in the country-side that was often highly syncretistic; the "ethical monotheism" of the classical prophets; the "Mosaic reform" of the Deuteronomistic school; and, finally, the post-Exilic priestly school with its religion of "ritual purity" (the foundation of later Judaism). Yet these various stages of religious development all tend to be combined in the final, idealized version that we have in the Hebrew Bible—almost as though Israelite religion had been handed down to Moses as a finished creation and did not undergo any subsequent change. Fortunately, the reworking and editing of the written sources has not completely obscured earlier materials that preserve alternate traditions, as we shall see.

The lateness of these texts is a fundamental limitation to our inquiry, not simply because the Biblical texts are secondary and to some degree artificial, but also because they are elitist. That is the result, in the first place, of the fact that the Hebrew Bible is a highly sophisticated literary creation which was written by and for the intelligentsia, who preserved, transmitted, and finally edited it into its present form. Such a document may reveal very little about the actual religion of the masses. For instance, we revere the lofty moral tone and the elegant prose of the book of Isaiah, but that does not address the question, if an individual prophet of that name had preached such sermons in the villages of Judah in the eighth century B.C., how would he have been understood and received? In the second place, the Hebrew Bible in its final redaction is almost exclusively the product of the Jerusalem priestly establishment and the royal court;

its Judaean "Davidic theology" was not typical of other traditions, such as that of northern Israel, for instance, much less of popular religion. We must always remember that what we happen to have preserved in the Bible is but a small residue of a much larger corpus of ancient Hebrew literature. It is obvious that the dominant literary school was royalist, not populist; and by and large only that tradition survives—though it was certainly not fully representative of ancient Israelite religious thought and practice. (Linguists have pointed out that even the language of the Bible preserves not the typical spoken Hebrew of the period, but largely the Judahite dialect, especially as it was cultivated in learned circles in Jerusalem.) As we shall see, however, archaeology brings to light other materials, both artifactual and written, that provide a fascinating comparison as well as a glimpse into popular religion.

Finally, the Hebrew Bible is limited as a historical source for reconstructing ancient Israelite religion in that much of it originates in priestly circles. Such circles are naturally concerned with portraying normative religion rather than actual religious practice—i.e., orthodoxy, not orthopraxy, much less heterodoxy. Not only is the resultant picture of Israelite religion a somewhat artificial reconstruction, but it tends to distort and even to suppress dissident theological views and religious practices condemned as deviant (if the latter are mentioned at all). In short, the Bible tells us a great deal about what, in the opinion of the Yahwistic writers, the ancient Israelites *ought* to have believed and practiced, and very little about what they actually did. Again, archaeology's greatest contribution to the study of Israelite religion lies in its potential for looking at the other side of the coin, at folk religion and the views of the counter-culture.[3]

Until recently scholars have been largely confined to the Hebrew Bible as the original source of information concerning Israelite religion, and this has naturally shaped the predominant views. There are three principal schools of thought, ways in which scholars have approached the material.

For more than a century now, the Biblical literature has been subjected to a minute and exhaustive analysis, using the tools of various modern schools of literary criticism. The earliest, *higher criticism*, or source and redaction criticism, analyzed larger blocks of literary material with regard to authorship, written documents or other sources, date of composition, and later editing. *Form criticism* explored the social setting and function of the various literary types and the history of their transmission. *Tradition history* sought the process of the earlier transmission of both oral and written traditions, that is, the larger units isolated by form criticism. *Textual* or *lower criticism* dealt with the handing down of the Biblical text once it had reached its penultimate and final written form, largely through analysis and comparison of differing versions. Finally, *redaction history* attempted to illuminate the intentions of the redactors, or editors, especially the final ones.[4]

For purposes of reconstructing Israelite religion, however, all these purely literary-critical analyses had limited value. Fragmentation of the texts became excessive, causing scholars to get lost in minutiae. Worse still, analysis became an end in itself. Even when scholarly consensus could be reached (which was rare), the result was often merely a history of the literature *about* the religion of Israel, rather than the actual history of that religion.

Biblical theology, though it may make use of some of the results of modern literary criticism (at least in its non-Fundamentalist versions), regards the Bible more as Scripture. Indeed, some scholars would argue that this approach is essentially the way the Biblical writers themselves used older material in seeking to systematize religious and moral teachings for the church and synagogue. In this view, Biblical theology is not a modern construct forced upon the ancient texts, for both its categories and its content derive from the Bible itself. For this reason, Biblical theology is usually distinguished from systematic or dogmatic theology (and implicitly regarded by some as more "normative").

The question remains, however, whether there *is* any real "theology" in the Hebrew Bible, at least in the modern sense that is usually implied, of unifying themes. The voluminous literature on Biblical theology in the last two hundred years reveals persistent attempts to revive this discipline with new emphases, but it also documents how controversial and ultimately frustrating this approach is. For instance, the main themes of the recent Biblical theology movement would seem to lend themselves to our inquiry concerning religion—especially its characteristic emphasis on the theological dimensions of the Bible, the religious uniqueness and relevance of ancient Israel, and the notion of the revelation of God in history. But upon reflection it becomes clear that most so-called "Old Testament theologies" are works of Christian apologetics; in the postwar era, they have been largely American, Protestant reactions to the classic Liberal Protestant theology of the earlier twentieth century. It is not without significance that virtually no Jewish scholars, and very few Roman Catholic scholars, have ever attempted to write a Biblical theology. The use of the Hebrew Bible as Christian Scripture, or even simply as a source book for modern theology and morality, may be legitimate. But we must separate very strictly the normative-theological task, which is a value judgment, from the more objective and basic descriptive-historical task, which is all that we are concerned with here, and all that archaeology can contribute. Biblical theology, like the literary-critical approach, may provide insights to guide research, but it is limited in apprehending ancient Israelite beliefs, much less actual religious practices, on their own terms.[5] What we seek to grasp if at all possible, is the *Ding an Sich*, the essential phenomenon, in its original context. We must postpone the question "What *does* Israelite religion mean?" until we first attempt to ascertain "What *did* it mean?," that is, "What *was* it?"

That leads us finally to a third approach, that of *Religionsgeschichte* or the "history of religions" school, the modern discipline of comparative religion. This school, which developed only in the late 19th century as archaeology brought to light parallel textual data from the Ancient Near East, adopts a basically historical approach. But it also attempts to move toward a true "science of religion" insofar as it employs empirical methods. While stressing, of course, the need for empathy on the part of the observer who seeks to grasp and to portray the essence of any ancient religion, this school focuses more on the need for objectivity, dispassionate analysis of the data, and comparative evaluation in the light of both other contemporary religions and modern ethnographic parallels. *Religionsgeschichte* may be characterized as phenomenological in that it concentrates on ancient religion itself, rather than on its modern relevance; and as functional, in that it emphasizes not just theoretical belief but the overall role religion plays in actually shaping society. Obviously, the *Religionsgeschichte* approach is much more compatible with archaeology than are the schools of literary criticism and Biblical theology when archaeology, as I shall demonstrate, seeks to illuminate ancient Israelite religious practice in its material and sociological setting.[6] I have attempted, in this study, to characterize modern archaeology as a parallel way of looking at the reality portrayed in the textual evidence. What specifically can archaeology contribute to an understanding of ancient Israelite religion, that texts cannot?[7]

First, archaeology alone supplies the general cultural background against which Israelite religion can be realistically portrayed, in particular the larger context in ancient Canaanite religion and culture in the second and first millennia B.C. This was the crucible in which Israel was forged, which shaped her distinctive life and institutions, without which she simply cannot be adequately understood. Yet it is only due to archaeological discoveries in this century that we have begun to resurrect the long-lost world of Canaanite history and culture—especially in the spectacular find of the library of fourteenth- to thirteenth-century B.C. cuneiform mythological texts from Ugarit. More recently, the systematic excavation of dozens of late Bronze Age sites in Israel, Jordan, and Syria has brought to light the rich and cosmopolitan material culture of Canaan in the two or three centuries just preceding the emergence of Israel. As shown in the previous chapter the entity we call "Israel" did not appear suddenly, or in a vacuum, but was born out of a long and bitter struggle with Canaanite culture that affected every aspect of life. The conflict between Baʿal and Yahweh was no sham battle, with the triumph of the God of Israel assured, but a crisis that threatened Israel's faith and indeed her very existence for centuries.[8]

Second, archaeology is uniquely equipped to illuminate actual religious practices, rather than simply the theological beliefs described in the texts, though admittedly some texts also deal with practice. Here, as previously, we must distinguish between normative religion—or what the orthodox establishment sought to enforce in the name of religion—and popular or folk religion, what the majority of people in fact believed and practiced. They are rarely the same, nor can we necessarily extrapolate one from the other. I have already suggested that the Biblical texts tend to supply an "official" version of Israelite religion; archaeology more often than not complements this highly idealized and homogenized picture by illuminating the varieties of actual religious practices, whether mentioned in the Bible or not. Religion is certainly a symbolic system, but textual references tend to abstract religion from the larger cultural context by intellectualizing it unduly. Modern archaeology focuses not chiefly on thought (which is, in any case, mostly beyond the reach of its techniques), but rather on the material correlates of individual human behavior, that is, the material remains that may reflect social and cultural patterning. In this area the texts fall short—particularly if they are elitist, as I have argued above. In short, if religion is what people do—not simply what theologians think—then archaeology can offer a complementary and perhaps occasionally superior view.

This leads to my third and final point: archaeology's unique contribution lies in its ability to illuminate certain aspects of the ancient cult, in particular popular piety and religious practice. Such folk religion may or may not correspond to the orthodox prescription preserved in the texts. But since it probably represents the majority opinion (or at least the prevalent expression in religious practice), it may be considered the true religion of ancient Israel—true, that is, from the phenomenological or functionalist perspective. I shall go on to discuss evidence that in a number of its features the so-called Israelite religion scarcely differed from the fertility religions of greater Canaan; and that in many quarters the cult of Yahweh was half pagan, not only in the period of the Judges but even until the end of the Monarchy.

The Evidence from Archaeology:
Material Remains of the Israelite Cult

A summary of some specific archaeological discoveries may provide a supplementary or perhaps an alternate view. First, I shall survey discoveries of Israelite shrines, which consist of either large open-air cult places or small domestic and household installations. Until recently no open-air sanctuaries had been discovered that were clearly identifiable as Israelite, although the numerous references in the Hebrew Bible to Canaanite "high places" suggested that we might expect to find parallel installations at Israelite sites of the twelfth and eleventh centuries B.C.

In 1981, Professor Amihai Mazar of the Hebrew University in Jerusalem followed up on the chance find of a magnificent bronze bull figurine and thus came to excavate a small isolated hilltop shrine five miles east of Dothan, in the heartland of Biblical Manasseh (see figure 15). The site featured only a large altar-like stone installation, with a few sherds of Iron I pottery and a tantalizing bronze fragment (figure 32). The "bull site," as it has come to be called, is almost certainly an Israelite open-air cult

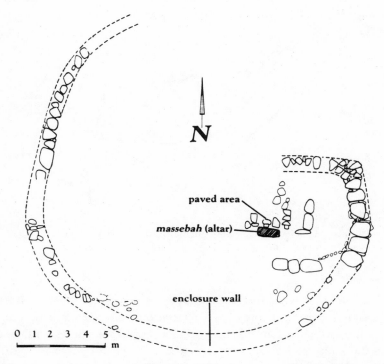

N

paved area

massebah (altar)

enclosure wall

0 1 2 3 4 5
m

Figure 32. Plan of the "Bull Site" (twelfth century B.C.). From A. Mazar, *BASOR* 247, fig. 5.

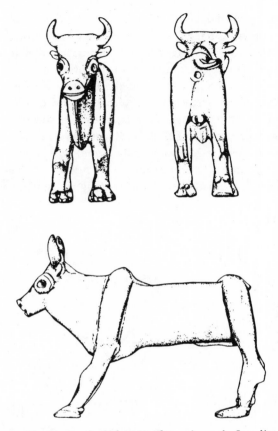

Figure 33. The bronze bull figurine from the early Israelite cult site.
From A. Mazar, *BASOR* 247, fig. 2.

place, probably what the Hebrew Bible means by the phrase *bāmāh*, or Canaanite-style "high place." As for the bull figurine itself (figure 33), it is irresistible to connect this with the worship of the god El, head of the Canaanite pantheon at Ugarit, whose principal epithet is "Bull" because of his fertility imagery (figure 34). This is the same El who appears in the oldest traditions in the Hebrew Bible (one of the two names for

Figure 34. Bronze statuettes of El, the chief Canaanite deity.

God, the other being Yahweh). He is seen especially in primitive name formulae in the patriarchal narratives, such as El-ʾolām, "El, the Eternal One"; El-shadday, "El, the Mountain One"; El-ʾelohê-Israel, "El, the god of Israel"; and the like. The discovery of the bull shrine lends strong support to the view of Prof. Frank Cross of Harvard, probably our foremost historian of early Israelite religion, that in the formative period Israelite Yahweh was still identified with El, the old high god of Canaan. As though to confirm that, the new Israelite bronze bull is almost identical to one excavated by Yadin some years ago at Hazor, from a Late Bronze Age Canaanite context some hundred to two hundred years earlier.[9]

By coincidence, the same year as the "bull site" was found, a second open-air shrine turned up, excavated (1982–84) by Adam Zertal of the Institute of Archaeology at Tel Aviv University. This shrine, located on Mt. Ebal just northwest of the Shechem pass, on the highest peak in northern Samaria, is dated by pottery fragments to the early Israelite (Iron I) period, ca. 1225–1100 B.C. The principal installation is a large, rectangular stone altar, approximately twenty-five by thirty feet, reached by an ascending ramp surrounded by a *temenos* (or enclosure wall) (figure 35).

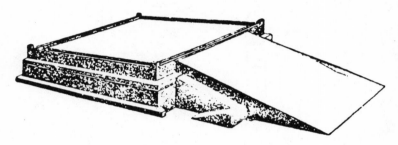

Figure 35. Schematic plan of the Mt. Ebal altar. From A. Zertal,
BAR II, no. 1:36.

Around the altar, and also under it (from an earlier phase), were small circular stone installations with quantities of burnt animal bones— mostly sheep, goat, young bulls, and fallow deer—evidently the remains of sacrificial offerings. Outside the altar there were other stone circles, some similar, but others with pottery and no burnt bones or ashes (figure 36). The pottery included not only the distinctive collar-rim store jars, but also jugs, chalices, a bit of common domestic pottery, and a number of small handmade ritual or votive vessels. Not surprisingly, the excavator has suggested that this late thirteenth- early twelfth-century B.C. installation may be the very altar built on Mt. Ebal by Joshua, which is described in Joshua 8:30–35 as having been built of unhewn stones and featuring burnt offerings to Yahweh. If this interpretation is

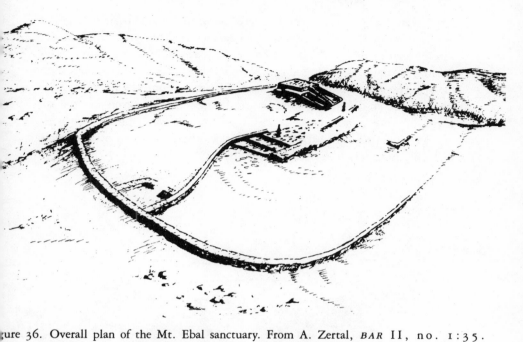

Figure 36. Overall plan of the Mt. Ebal sanctuary. From A. Zertal, *BAR* II, no. 1:35.

confirmed by more evidence, it will be a rare case of archaeology having turned up a long-lost cultic installation specifically mentioned in the Bible. [10]

Another possible case would be the ninth-century B.C. "high place" excavated in the 1970s by Avraham Biran at Tel Dan. According to I Kings 12:25–31, when Jeroboam seceded from Judah and the Jerusalem temple upon Solomon's death, he established a new center for the separate kingdom of Israel at Dan, where he set up a rival sanctuary with a golden calf and "made houses on high places." The latter expression, *beth bāmôt*, is enigmatic; but it may refer to some sort of structure built atop a *bāmāh*, i.e., on a platform or Canaanite-style high place of the sort mentioned in several Biblical passages. The Dan structure is a large, magnificent stone platform approximately sixty feet square, approached by a flight of steps (figure 37). It may be interpreted as simply an open-air high place or platform, or alternatively as the foundation for either a tabernacle structure or a more permanent building, such as a temple. If the latter, then we may actually have located Jeroboam's "house [i.e., temple] on a high place." The cultic nature of the Dan structure is confirmed by finds made in the vicinity, including a miniature horned altar, a seven-spouted oil lamp, offering stands, bronze shovels and implements, human figurines, and an olive pressing installation similar to those found in other temple or shrine precincts (see figure 38 and below).[11]

Figure 37. The "high place" at Dan (ninth century B.C.). From *Encyclopedia of Archaeological Excavations in the Holy Land*, Vol. I, p. 319.

We now have a number of smaller Israelite domestic area or household shrines, all intramural and perhaps for private or familial worship. Some have been known for some time, but only recently have they been correctly understood. A group of artifacts discovered in the 1930s in the courtyard of Building 2081 of Stratum VA at Megiddo from the time of Solomon, includes two stone horned altars, ceramic cultic stands, chalices, and other vessels. This is almost certainly an Israelite household shrine, where animal, other food and drink, and perhaps incense offerings were made.[12] At nearby Ta'anach, a contemporary cult installation was

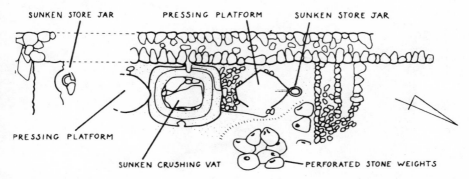

Figure 38. Plan of the olive-pressing installation in the temple precincts at Dan (ninth century B.C.?). From L. A. Stager and S. R. Wolff, *BASOR* 243, fig. 1.

found in the domestic quarter, with spectacular finds that are only now beginning to be fully appreciated. In the 1960s Paul W. Lapp excavated a "Cultic Structure," a tenth-century B.C. two-room building, whose main feature was another basin or oil press, like that at Dan (figure 39). From this building also came clear cultic artifacts, such as a mold for casting Asherah or Astarte Mother-Goddess figurines (see below); some sixty loom weights, evidence of weaving in temple precincts, such as that attested elsewhere and also in the Bible (cf. II Kings 23:7); and 140 sheep and goat astragali (knuckle bones), often found in cultic contexts. The most astonishing find was a large, square terra-cotta offering stand, closely resembling one found sixty years earlier by German excavators on the same spot. It features not only the sun disc and the sacred tree of life on the upper registers, but also a pair of lionesses; on the lower registers there are scenes of human-headed lionesses, and also a nude female grasping two lionesses by the ears (figure 40).[13]

Few scholars have commented on the remarkable iconography of this Israelite offering stand. But there is growing evidence that the female figure is none other than the Mother Goddess Asherah, consort of El and the great goddess of sex and fertility in Canaan, one of whose principal epithets was "the Lion Lady." In Egypt, she is often portrayed nude, astride a lion (figure 41). From Palestine, we have several twelfth- or

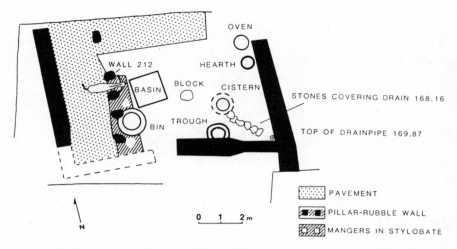

Figure 39. Plan of the Taʿanach "Cultic Structure" (tenth century B.C.). From P. W. Lapp, *BASOR* 173, fig. 12.

eleventh-century B.C. arrowheads, inscribed with the names of archers dedicated to "the Lion Lady." On the altar of an early Iron I temple at Jaffa there was found the perfectly preserved skull of a lioness, and at contemporary temples at nearby Tell Qasile several lion-headed masks and *rhyta* (drinking vessels) turned up. There is no doubt in my mind that just as Canaanite El could be worshipped in early Israel, so could his consort Asherah, often in the guise of Hathor or the "Lion Lady." Even more striking evidence from the period of the divided Monarchy will be discussed below.[14]

Another tenth-century B.C. Israelite domestic shrine was found at Tell el-Farʿah (N.), Biblical Tirzah, by the late Pére Roland de Vaux in the 1950s. This is a small structure near the city gate, again featuring an oil pressing installation. This was not properly understood until 1981, when a brilliant article by Lawrence Stager and Samuel Wolff brought together all the above evidence and demonstrated that a particularly fine quality of olive oil for cultic use was often manufactured right in temple precincts, precisely as suggested in several Biblical passages.[15]

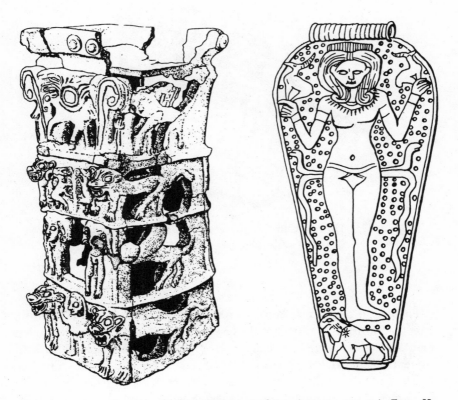

Figure 40. The Taᶜanach ceramic offering stand (tenth century B.C.). From K. Galling, ed., *Biblisches Realexicon*, 2d edition, fig. 45.

Figure 41. Gold plaque portraying a nude Asherah astride a lion; the goddess has the typical Hathor-wig and grasps an ibex (often a lotus or snake) in each hand (Late Bronze Age, fourteenth-thirteenth century B.C.). From O. Negbi, *Canaanite Gods in Metal*, fig. 118.

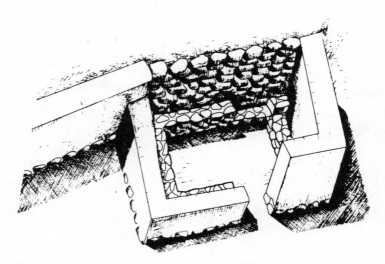

Figure 42. Plan of "Cult Room 49" at Lachish (tenth century B.C.).
From Y. Aharoni et al., *Lachish* V, fig. 7.

Finally, in the 1960s, Yohanan Aharoni discovered at Judean Lachish
a tenth-century B.C. Israelite shrine, Cult Room 49. This small single-
room structure featured low benches for offerings around three walls. The
contents included several small horned altars, ceramic stands, libation
bowls, and other ceramic vessels (figure 42). Here we have another Israelite domestic or private cult installation, in which food or drink offerings
were presented.[16]

It may be significant that all the public open-air or domestic-household
shrines discovered thus far in Israel are early—twelfth- to tenth-century
B.C., that is, dating only down to the time of the early Monarchy. According to the Biblical tradition, worship was then centralized in Jerusalem by Solomon, in connection with the construction of the great Temple
and the establishment of the Jerusalem priesthood under royal patronage.
While this policy of centralization was not universally enforced (as determined from archaeological discoveries which will be discussed below), the

relative lack of cult installations does suggest that many local shrines were suppressed in the late tenth century B.C. and thereafter.

The famous Solomonic Temple in Jerusalem is described in copious detail in 1 Kings 6–7, as well as in Ezekiel's dream of the restored Temple (Ezekiel 40–43). Yet not a trace of this splendid building has been turned up in a century and a half of concentrated archaeological work in Jerusalem. Nor is it ever likely to, since the First Temple was destroyed by the Babylonians in 587–86 B.C., and later razed to bedrock by Roman engineers for the construction of the Second Temple in Herodian times. And of course there is no possibility of scientific investigation at what is now the site of the Dome of the Rock and the al-Aqsa mosques—the third holiest shrine of Islam and an area proscribed for Orthodox Jews until the coming of the Messiah. Nonetheless, by studying archaeological discoveries at other sites, we can illustrate many details of the architectural plan and furnishings of the Solomonic Temple described in the Bible (cf. chapter 3).

Another significant shrine was discovered by the late Yohanan Aharoni during excavations of a small Israelite fortress at Arad, in the Negev desert northeast of Beersheba (1962–69). Here he found in Stratum XI a typical Solomonic casemate wall system enclosing an area whose principal architectural feature was a bipartite (two-room) temple. This is generally regarded as the only Israelite temple ever found by archaeologists. The plan goes back to local Canaanite prototypes of the early to mid-second millennium B.C., of which we now have several examples. The outer room at Arad was really a large open courtyard featuring a free-standing stone and mudbrick altar, around which were found burnt animal bones. Also found at the foot of the altar (in later Stratum X) were two shallow offering plates inscribed with the letters *qof kaf*, probably an abbreviation for *qōdeš kōhānîm*, "set apart for the priests."

The inner room (the *hekhal* of the Solomonic temple) had low benches for offerings around the walls and a niche at the back wall, reached by three steps. This niche, which was barely large enough to accommodate one person, differed from the inner chamber or "Holy of Holies" in the Solomonic temple, the *devîr* (where the High Priest entered once a year), by being much more accessible to the worshippers. Flanking this niche at the entrance were two small stone altars with traces of an organic, incense-like substance, and at the back wall there was a smoothed stone stela or monolith. This temple continued in use, with certain alterations, into Stratum VIII of the late eighth century B.C., when it was abolished, perhaps in the well-known reforms of King Hezekiah, who attempted to reestablish centralized worship in Jerusalem.

The Arad temple has been surrounded by controversy from the beginning, partly because of questions of date and interpretation arising from inadequate excavation and publication. But there is more to it than that. A number of prominent archaeologists and Bible scholars have tried to minimize the structure's importance, regarding it as merely a local shrine (i.e., neither a real temple nor comparable to the plan of the Solomonic temple) or even denying that it is Israelite. Aharoni himself compared the Arad structure to the descriptions of the Biblical tabernacle, rather than to the Solomonic temple. But when all the stratigraphic difficulties, theological presuppositions, and semantic confusions of previous discussions are put aside, it is evident that we have at Arad a full-fledged local Israelite temple. It functioned in the tenth through eighth centuries B.C. with its own priesthood and sacrificial offering system—despite the Deuteronomistic historian's proscription of such temples, and despite the fact that they were anathema to reforming kings and prophets.[17]

A more recent and even more astonishing find is the small Israelite sanctuary at Kuntillet ʿAjrûd, excavated by Ze'ev Meshel (1976–78). This is an eighth-century B.C. caravanserai, or stopover station, near springs on the trade routes through the eastern Sinai desert, about halfway between the oasis at Kadesh-barnea and the gulf of Eilat (figure 43). The single hilltop structure is a composite fort-hostel, with shelter and provisions for travelers. At the entrance is a two-room structure with plastered benches and side repositories, evidently a small sanctuary (figure 44). Painted on the walls here and elsewhere were numerous Hebrew inscriptions, one of the largest collections ever found anywhere. Few have yet been published, but one read "May Yahweh favor." Another, however, read "Blessed by Baʿal in the day ——— [illegible] the name of El in the day ———," with Canaanite Baʿal and El in parallelism. A large stone

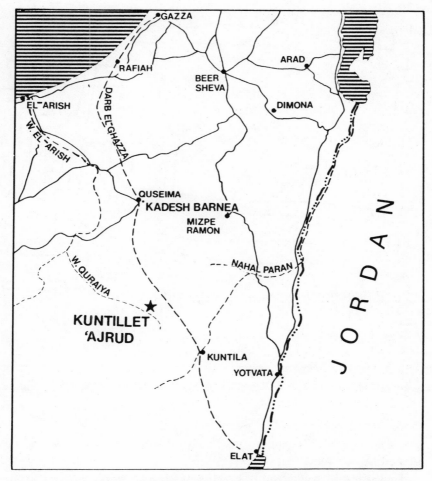

Figure 43. Map showing the location of Kuntillet ʿAjrûd (Ḥorvat Teiman).
From P. Beck, *Tel Aviv* 9, fig. 1.

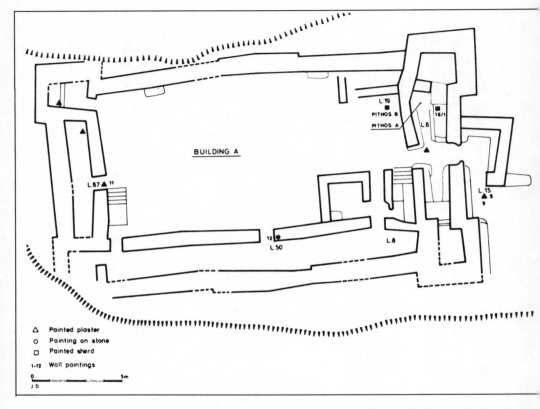

Figure 44. Plan of the fort at Kuntillet ʿAjrûd. From P. Beck, *Tel Aviv* 9, fig. 2.

votive bowl reads "Belonging to ʿOvadyau, son of ʿAdnah. May he be blessed by Yahweh."[18]

These hints of syncretism in Israelite worship are mild, however, compared to the scenes painted on a number of large store jars. First, there are familiar Phoenician motifs such as the cow suckling her calf, the sacred tree of life, and lions—all common enough themes in Israelite iconography, as witnessed by ivory carvings and seals of the period (figure 45). There is also a strange processional scene showing worshippers approach-

Figure 45. Scenes painted on one of the large ʿAjrûd storejars.
From P. Beck, *Tel Aviv* 9, fig. 4.

Figure 46. The ʿAjrûd processional scene. From P. Beck, *Tel Aviv* 9, fig. 6.

ing a deity, unfortunately not fully preserved on a broken store jar (figure 46). But the *pièce de résistance* is the scene on one large store jar which features, among other things, two representations of the Egyptian ithyphallic dwarf-god Bes, patron of music and dancing, guardian of the other gods, and in general an apotropaic or "good luck" deity. At the upper right there is a seated, half-nude female figure, holding a stringed lyre in her outstretched arms (figure 47). Who is she, our "Lady of ʿAjrûd"? The Hebrew inscription running across the top of the scene, which is perfectly legible, is another blessing formula, ending with the phrase "I bless you by Yahweh our guardian [*or* Yahweh of Samaria] and by his Asherah." In a recent article (cited below) I have pointed out that the female figure's chair is really a stylized lion-throne of the type often associated with kings and deities of the ancient Near East (figure 48) and, furthermore, that there are very close parallels to such seated female deities at Canaanite Ugarit (figure 49). Thus we should read the ʿAjrûd inscription literally: this actually is a representation of the Canaanite goddess, explicitly iden-

Figure 47. Hebrew inscription and scene on an ʿAjrûd storejar.
From Z. Meshel, *Kuntillet ʿAjrûd*, fig. 12.

tified as Asherah, and possibly thought of as the consort of Yahweh, the god of Israel!

Now in the Ugaritic texts, Asherah is the consort of El, the head of the pantheon; she is a symbol of sex and fertility, the great "Mother Goddess" of Canaan. The term *asherah* occurs some forty times in the Hebrew Bible. There, however, the writers have in most occurrences softened its impact by construing the term not as the personal name of a Canaanite deity, but rather as merely a cult symbol—a wooden pole (phallic sym-

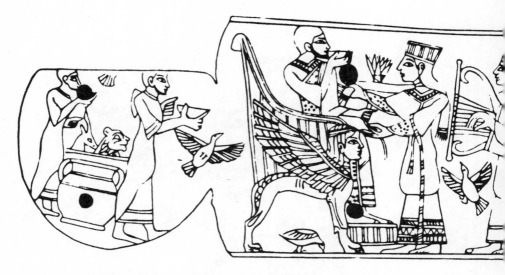

Figure 48. A Megiddo carved ivory panel with a processional before a lion-throne

Figure 49. Two electrum pendants from Ugarit, showing a female deity sitting on a stylized lion-throne (fourteenth century B.C.). From C. F. A. Schaeffer, *Ugaritica* I, figs. 149:1, 4.

(thirteenth-twelfth century B.C.). From G. Loud, *The Megiddo Ivories*, Plate 4:2b.

bol?) that the Israelites are said to have cut down and burnt as an abomination. Yet there are several texts mentioning "Ba'al and Asherah," in which the reference can only be to the Canaanite goddess herself. There are admissions in such passages as 2 Kings 21:7 and 23:7 that there were furnishings for Asherah in use even in the temple in Jerusalem. But the absence of extra-Biblical texts or archaeological evidence referring unequivocally to the goddess Asherah has rendered these texts without context, and therefore suspicious. My recent article concluded that

> The "silence" regarding Asherah as the consort of Yahweh, successor to Canaanite El, may now be understood as the result of the near-total suppression of the cult by the eighth- to sixth-century reformers. As a result, references to "Asherah," while not actually expunged from the consonantal text of the OT, were misunderstood by later editors or reinterpreted to suggest merely the shadowy image of the goddess. In this "innocent deception," they were followed by the translators of the Septuagint, the Vulgate, the

Targumim, and the King James and most other modern versions, including the Revised Standard. Indeed, by the time of the Mishna the original significance of the name "Asherah" had probably been forgotten, not to be recovered until the goddess emerged again in the texts recovered from Ugarit. Yet the very fact of the necessity for reform in ancient Israel reminds us that the worship of Asherah, the Mother Goddess, sometimes personified as the consort of Yahweh, was popular until the end of the Monarchy. The archaeological record has preserved for us an alternate version of events as portrayed in the received text—parallel, but not necessarily contradictory. Indeed, ʿAjrûd and el-Qôm enhance our appreciation of the prophetic message, for they provide for the first time a milieu in which we may understand just how crucial a threat the worship of the Canaanite fertility goddesses actually was.[19]

My interpretation of the ʿAjrûd evidence is, of course, somewhat controversial. All along Israeli scholars have been uncomfortable and have therefore taken a "minimalist" position, which in my opinion robs this rich material of its full significance. (Indeed, the scene on the store jar was not even published, or displayed clearly in the Israel Museum for a very long time.) Biblical scholars in Europe and America are only now beginning to confront the ʿAjrûd evidence, and they too seem reluctant to face the clear implication: that here at ʿAjrûd—far from the watchful eyes of the Jerusalem religious establishment and brought to light only by the accident of archaeological discovery—we have a half-pagan Israelite temple, where both Baʿal and Asherah could be worshipped alongside Yahweh.[20]

The new ʿAjrûd evidence really only confirms what was suspected fifteen years ago. In 1970 I published a badly defaced Hebrew inscription from an eighth-century B.C. Judean tomb that I had excavated at Kh. el-Qôm, west of Hebron. Although at the time only a handful of such inscriptions were known, it attracted little attention. Recently, however, thanks to the Asherah reference at ʿAjrûd, new meaning can be drawn from a previously misunderstood phrase in line three of the el-Qôm inscription (figure 50). There is today growing scholarly consensus that the phrase, "Blessed be ʿUriyahu by Yahweh, and from his enemies save him by his Asherah" must be interpreted exactly as at ʿAjrûd. Whether one accepts that these texts refer to the goddess herself, it is clear that someone or something

Figure 50. Inscription III from Kh. el-Qôm (eighth century B.C.).
From A. Lemaire, *Revue biblique* 84, fig. 1.

called "asherah" could be invoked in ancient Israel as an agent of blessing, regularly and without embarrassment.[21] Yet without data obtained by modern archaeology, we would never have known that. The Bible had suppressed the evidence.

In the study of Israelite shrines and temples, analysis of religious practice is largely limited to extrapolation from the basic architectural plan. But there is other archaeological evidence, perhaps more direct, in the furnishings and equipment, i.e., the religious paraphernalia found in these and other Israelite cultic contexts. Although some of this evidence has long been known, it has rarely been put together, much less adequately interpreted as reflecting Israelite religious practice. Here I can barely suggest the range and richness of this evidence.

I have already mentioned the smalled horned altars discovered at certain domestic shrines. There are, however, many other similar examples—so many that it is easy to conclude that small horned altars were common at Israelite sites from the tenth to the seventh century B.C. (figure 51). Horned altars are, in fact, mentioned in several Biblical texts, but the small altars previously unearthed did nothing to illuminate the peculiar Biblical descriptions of people "clinging to the horns of an altar" for safety. These texts made little sense until the first full-sized altar turned up, just a few years ago, during Aharoni's excavations at Beersheba (figure 52). It measures approximately six feet square, and is constructed of

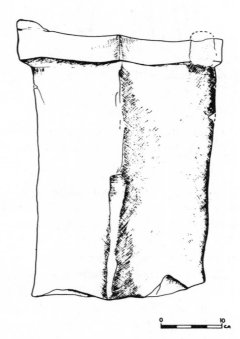

Figure 51. Small limestone "horned altar" from "Cult Room 49" at Lachish (tenth century B.C.). From Y. Aharoni, *Lachish V, The Sanctuary and Residency*, Plate 43:7.

well-dressed masonry with distinct carved horns at the four corners. This
was the first archaeological confirmation of Biblical references to the legal
custom by which people could claim sanctuary by "clinging to the horns"
of a large altar, as Adonijah did in David's sanctuary or as the Israelites
are said to have done earlier in the "cities of refuge." The masonry blocks
of the Beersheba altar were actually found dismantled and incorporated
into the rubble fill of a later building. As Aharoni suggested quite plausi-
bly, the deliberate destruction of the Beersheba altar was possibly the
work of King Hezekiah in the late eighth century B.C., among whose
reform measures was an attempt to abolish the local sanctuaries, which

Figure 52. The large "horned altar" from Beersheba, as reassembled
(eighth or seventh century B.C.). From *BAR* II, no. 1:38.

had undoubtedly become partly pagan. Of Hezekiah it was said, "He removed the high places, and broke the pillars, and cut down the Asherah" (2 Kings 18:4).[22]

In addition to the evidence for monumental or other "horned" altars in ancient Israel, we also know of miniature limestone household altars, almost certainly for incense, some elaborately decorated. These are mostly rather late in date, beginning in the seventh century B.C. or so, and continuing in use in Israelite circles through at least the Persian and Hellenistic periods.

We have looked only briefly at the ceramic stands, of which we now have numerous Israelite examples (figure 53). These have usually been called "incense stands" because of the fenestrated column, through whose

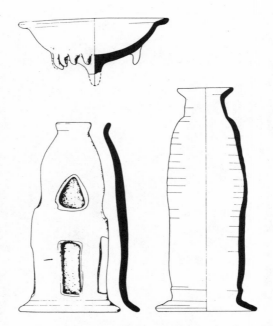

Figure 53. Ceramic cult stands and libation bowls from "Cult Room 49" at Lachish (tenth century B.C.). From Y. Aharoni, *Lachish V: The Sanctuary and the Residence*, plates 43:1–4.

openings one could imagine the smoke of incense wafting. Practically speaking, however, the stands are not really suitable for incense. A better interpretation would be that these are stands for libation offerings, as indeed the attached but removable bowls on some examples attest. Presumably, then, the stands were used for presenting wine, oil, or other liquid offerings, as prescribed in many Biblical passages. (They could, of course, be used for dry food offerings as well.) The fenestrations on other stands suggest not smoke vents but windows, and these stands may therefore belong to a class of "temple models" (see below), some of which are adorned with fantastic bas-reliefs of serpents, lions, the tree of life, and other symbols of the deities. The Ta'anach stand discussed above is certainly of this type (though of course the top of such a stand could also be used for gifts of food, drink, or even incense). Still other stands may be stylized versions of the familiar tree of life, one of the oldest and most widespread motifs in ancient Near Eastern art and iconography. In any case, it is clear that all these supposedly Israelite cult stands are borrowed, almost without alteration, from much older, pre-Israelite prototypes, of which we now have many examples; and further that they are mostly connected with the food and drink offerings typical of the Canaanite fertility cults.[23]

That there also existed a separate class of temple models, however, is now seen in a number of unpublished or recently published terra-cotta examples (figure 54). Some of these feature tree-of-life columns, doves, or lionesses (the latter, symbols connected with the goddess Asherah). A number of these house or temple models come from Trans-Jordan and are probably Moabite or Edomite. But recently an indisputably Israelite example from the ninth century B.C. was published from Tell el-Far'ah, Biblical Tirzah, which for a brief time was the capital of northern Israel. These temple models or miniature "houses of the gods" were no doubt household shrines, but exactly how they functioned we do not know.[24]

We come now to an intriguing class of "magic" vessels, small ceramic artifacts that are almost certainly cultic, but whose exact use is unknown. We have a number of ceramic "rattles," which may of course be only toys, but alternatively may have been used in the musical ceremonies that are well attested in both the Canaanite and Israelite cult. More interesting,

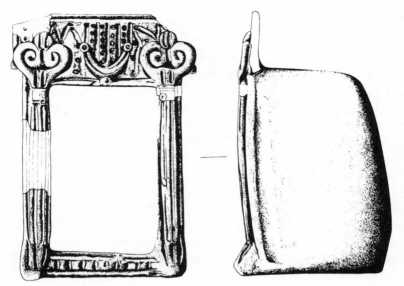

Figure 54. Terra-cotta temple model from (ca. Tell el-Far‹ah (N.) ninth century B.C.). From A. Chambon, *Tel el-Far‹ah* I: *L'Age du Fer*, plate 66.

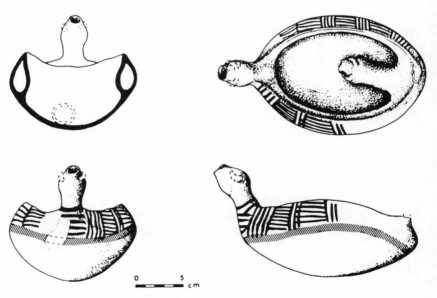

Figure 55. *Kernos* from Tell Qasile (twelfth-eleventh century B.C.).

but also more mysterious, are the *kernoi*, or "trick vessels." These are small bowls that have a hollow rim, to which are attached one or more pouring spouts, usually in the shape of animal heads but sometimes models of pomegranates or other fruits (figure 55). These amusing vessels can be manipulated so as to pour liquids in various ways, but they are surely not simply toys and must have been used for libation offerings. Again, the several Israelite examples we have from the tenth to eighth centuries B.C. are derived from "foreign" prototypes—in this case twelfth- and eleventh-century B.C. Philistine examples. Behind these, in turn, lies a Cypriot tradition—not surprising since the Philistines were one of the groups of Sea Peoples who immigrated to the coast of Palestine in the early Iron Age, where they came into contact with the Israelites. Just why these *kernoi* were adopted by the Israelites, or how they functioned in the Israelite cult, is uncertain.[25]

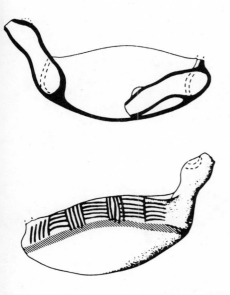

From A. Mazar, *Excavations at Tel Qasile, Part I*, fig. 39.

Among the most common finds at Israelite sites are small terra-cotta figurines, both zoomorphic and anthropomorphic. The representations of animals (figure 56) are mostly large quadrupeds, especially horses and young bulls, but one also finds smaller animals, in one case a delightful three-legged chicken. The horses are often shown with a bridle and sad-

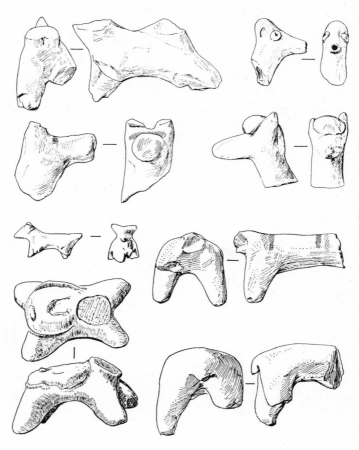

Figure 56. Zoomorphic figurines from Jerusalem (eighth-seventh century B.C.). From K. M. Kenyon, *Jerusalem. Excavating* 3000 *Years of History*, fig. 9.

dle, and many of them have a human mount. A high proportion of these Israelite zoomorphic vessels come from tombs, and many of them are hollow with filling and pouring devices similar to those of the *kernoi*. This would suggest that they, too, were used for libations, in this case perhaps offerings in connection with the burial of the dead. Other animal figurines are solid, mostly handmade and either crudely or very schematically modelled; some of these have what appears to be a solar disc on the head, reminiscent of the pagan sun-cult iconography of the period (cf. 2 Kings 23:11). I can offer no explanation of the reason for or the choice of the animal motifs, except to note that the Canaanite goddesses Asherah and ʿAnat appear astride horses on plaques of the preceding Late Bronze period. However, in Israelite agricultural villages, the modeling of common farm animals in clay was probably a natural impulse, so not all of the zoomorphic figurines need be interpreted cultically.

The human figurines are also problematic. Thousands of these terra cottas have been found at Israelite sites, in all kinds of contexts: domestic, cultic, and funerary. The striking thing is that virtually all of these figurines are female; there is scarcely a single clear example of a male figurine, bronze or ceramic, from an Israelite site. It had been supposed all along that the so-called Astarte figurines are representations of the great Mother Goddess of Canaan, especially since most show the female form nude, with exaggerated breasts (figure 57); occasionally she is depicted pregnant or nursing a child . The features of these Iron Age *Dea Nutrix* figurines are very similar to those of the preceding Late Bronze Age, which are usually assumed to be representations of the Canaanite goddess of sex and fertility, Asherah, ʿAnat, or Astarte. Now the more blatantly sexual motifs give way to the nursing mother. This suggests that here again we have evidence of the direct borrowing of features from the Canaanite cult of the Mother Goddess. The lack of any male figurines in Israel would then be explained by the explicit prohibition in the second commandment; modeling or invoking the familiar Mother Goddess might be permissible in a rite concerning conception, childbirth, or lactation, but portraying Yahweh himself in this fashion would be unthinkable.

Despite the obvious connection of the female figurines with the fertility cults of Canaan, many scholars have taken the "minimalist" view that no

Figure 57. "Astarte" (Asherah) figurine of the pillar-base type (eighth-seventh century B.C.). From N. Avigad, *Discovering Jerusalem*, fig. 15.

particular deity can be identified in these figurines; that is, they are simply talismans that Israelite women used without necessarily being aware of the significance of the female representation. It had also been supposed that these figurines were typical only of folk religion and thus had little significance in the official Israelite cult. But the discovery of the ʿAjrûd sanctuary and the related textual evidence noted above demonstrates beyond reasonable doubt that Asherah could be named, and even worshipped, in ancient Israel. Thus there is no longer any reason in my mind to hesitate about identifying these as "Asherah figurines" (although be-

cause of the well-known coalescence of the three Canaanite fertility goddesses, they could also represent ʿAnat or Astarte).[26] As for the notion that
these figurines, whatever they signified, were uncommon in orthodox circles, the late Dame Kathleen Kenyon found a seventh-century B.C. "cult-
cache" with more than three-hundred-fifty of them in a cave in Jerusalem,
not a hundred yards from the Temple Mount (figure 58). It is tempting
to see in these figurines dramatic evidence of the background of reforms

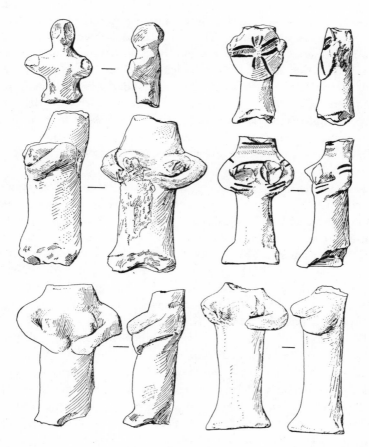

Figure 58. Female figurines from Kenyon's "cult-cache" in Jerusalem (seventh century B.C.). From K. M. Kenyon, *Jerusalem*, fig. 10.

such as that of King Josiah, who it is said in 2 Kings 23:4 "brought out of the temple of the Lord all the vessels made for Ba'al and for Asherah and . . . burned them outside Jerusalem."[27]

An almost entirely overlooked resource for reconstructing Israelite religion lies in the art and iconography of the period, most of which is clearly not secular. Our principal evidence for Israelite art comes from the Monarchy (ninth-seventh century B.C.), in the form of seals, or engraved gem stones for signet rings, and richly carved ivory inlays for fine furniture. There is so much material that in this survey I can only illustrate it briefly and hint at its significance. The hundreds of known Hebrew seals and seal impressions are of two classes: those with private name formulae, which are a rich source for the ancient Israelite onomasticon; and those with pictorial representations (figure 59). The latter are almost without exception in the Phoenician style, the hallmark of which is the combination of bungled Egyptian and Mesopotamian motifs. The favorite themes are scarabeus beetles, uraeus serpents, the tree of life, lions, and other animals; human representations are rare on Hebrew seals, and deities are unknown.[28]

The contemporary ivories are also mostly Phoenician in style, with many of the same motifs as the seals. In addition, however, they have many more standard Egyptian and Assyrian scenes, such as "the infant Horus sitting on a lotus blossom," the sphinx, the "cow suckling her calf," the "woman at the window," and especially various stylized trees of life. The best collection of these Phoenician-style ivories comes from the ruins of the palace of Ahab at the Israelite capital of Samaria (figure 60). This illustrates more than anything else how easily "pagan" art was incorporated into the "official" Israelite cult.[29]

It must be stressed that none of the seal or ivory motifs is distinctively "Israelite"; all are borrowed from surrounding cultures. We may argue, of course, that this artistic borrowing does not necessarily mean that the Israelites consciously adopted the religious symbolism of the iconography of these seals, much less the pagan deities of other cultures. It is obvious, however, that Israelite art—so expressive and reflective a medium of culture—was almost wholly derivative. This fact lends support to the

Figure 59. A selection of Israelite and Judean seals (eighth-seventh century B.C.)

Figure 60. Carved ivory inlays from Ahab's palace at Samaria, in Phoenician style (ninth-eighth century B.C.). From J. W. Crowfoot, J. M. Crowfoot, and K. M. Kenyon, *Samaria-Sebaste* II, plates 5, 6, 17, 22.

general hypothesis that many aspects of Israelite religion were also borrowed. Even where possibly transformed by Yahwistic theology, these symbols and practices never quite lost their pagan connotations—especially in popular religion, where unsophisticated folk did not draw fine distinctions and so were always inclined to syncretism.

On Reconstructing Ancient Israelite Religious Belief and Practice

This brief survey can only hint at the rich archaeological resources now at our disposal for reconstructing ancient Israelite religious practice. Yet any survey of the standard treatments of Israelite history and religion during the past thirty years would show that Biblical scholars have made scant and largely inept use of the archaeological data. The ultimate irony is that even the Biblical archaeology movement, which sought to combine Palestinian archaeology and theological studies, made little contribution to the elucidation of Israelite religion—as witness the fact that Wright's own interpretation of an actual Israelite temple he excavated at the tribal league center of Shechem has been either rejected or, increasingly, ignored altogether.[30] In short, the archaeological revolution in Biblical studies predicted by Albright in the 1930s is not over: it has never really begun. How can one explain this curious failure of Biblical scholars to utilize archaeological discoveries—especially when the public is endlessly fascinated by these same discoveries?

The reasons are many. First, recent scholarly hesitation may be due in part to a reaction against the extremes of earlier Biblical archaeology, which labeled as "cultic" any archaeological feature that could not otherwise be explained. Thus every large standing stone became a maṣṣēbāh, every flat lying stone an altar. The popular handbooks are filled with such scandalous nonsense, which serious scholars rightly reject. Unfortunately, this amateurism and sensationalism have done so much lasting damage to our branch of archaeology that many Biblical historians want nothing more to do with it, even though Syro-Palestinian archaeology has now become quite professional. Second, there is the sheer difficulty that nonspecialists, even when interested, face in keeping up with the fast-moving theoretical trends, the phenomenal accumulation of new data, and the proliferation of literature in archaeology. And the failure of archaeologists to interpret and publish adequately does not help.

But there are more significant intellectual reasons why the subject of archaeology and the cult is neglected. One is that many of the Protestant

Biblical scholars, both European and American, who have dominated the field of Old Testament studies and Palestinian archaeology apparently have had a profound bias against the very notion of "cult." The whole Reformation orientation was toward the proclamation of the Word of God, rather than the Sacraments, with the result that these Protestant scholars turned naturally to intellectual formulations, rather than ritual or symbol—to theology, not the practice of religion. A close examination of the vast literature on Old Testament theology will show, I believe, not only neglect of the Israelite cult, but a certain repugnance—even for the term "cult," which is often used negatively. The same repugnance, however, is seen in much modern Jewish scholarship, even Orthodoxy, which after all has abolished the ancient Israelite sacrificial cult. Archaeology, however, with its emphasis on actual religious practice, provides a healthy corrective to this fastidiousness, this over-intellectualization of religion that may rob it of its true power and vitality. In any case, such an approach lacks the empathy to bring us close enough to understand the ancient Israelite cult.

Recent archaeological discoveries have cast particularly interesting and surprising light on the identification of various deities and rituals in ancient Israel. Yahweh, the god of Israel, was unattested outside the Bible until modern research and excavation placed this deity in the context of ancient Near Eastern history and religion through parallel textual discoveries, including the first actual occurrence of the name "Yahweh" in Hebrew inscriptions only a few years ago. But archaeology now confirms (as the Bible hints) that other deities, specifically Canaanite fertility gods, were revered in ancient Israel. Chief among them were the "Mother Goddess" Asherah, as we saw above, and the "Storm God" Ba'al, whom the Israelites apparently regarded as her consort. ('Anat, Ba'al's consort at Ugarit, plays a minor role in the Hebrew Bible, although she is mentioned, and indeed she is attested in archaeology as well.) Thus it is clear that in ancient Israel, until the Exile, Asherah and Ba'al were not shadowy numina, dead and discredited gods of old Canaan. Rather, the pair were potent rivals of Yahweh himself, and for the masses their cult, with its promise of integration with the very life-giving forces of Nature, remained an attractive alternative to the more austere religion and ethical demands of Yahwism.

Archaeological illumination of the pervasiveness of the Canaanite fertility cults in Israel is not revolutionary; actually, it merely confirms what the Bible suggests—but downplays. Indeed, archaeology only brings to the surface a strong undercurrent throughout the Hebrew Bible: the eloquent prophetic protest against the ever-present threat of idolatry. Archaeology supplies the social and religious context of the period. In short, it demonstrates that the prophets knew what they were talking about.

It has long been suspected that the early Israelite cult was monolatrous, but certainly not monotheistic in the philosophical sense. This syncretistic cult can now be illustrated directly by archaeological finds that antedate most of the Biblical texts, and therefore constitute primary evidence. A summary of the discoveries discussed above, taken together with the texts in Joshua, Judges, and Samuel, shows that the primary features of the pre-Monarchic Israelite cult were as follows: (1.) Worship was a localized affair, with open-air sanctuaries or even simple household shrines serving most ordinary folk in everyday practice. There were few, if any, actual temples, and no centralized worship. (2.) In the rarity of elaborate clerical or priestly institutions, any individual Israelites (males at least) could officiate in worship. Anyone could build an altar, plant a sacred tree, erect a stela, or offer sacrifices—the characteristic (and probably exclusive) cultic activities. (3.) The most prominent rituals were simply the frequent presentation of food and drink offerings—grains, cereals, olive oil, wine and sacrifices of sheep or goats—the principal agricultural products of Canaan centuries before the appearance of the Israelites. (4.) There may have been more periodic public festivals; the ones that we know of were also borrowed from Canaan and followed the Canaanite agricultural year. These were: the spring pastoral feast, when lambs were slaughtered, identified quite naturally by Israelites with the Passover (or Pesach), when their first-born were spared in Egypt; the early summer agriculture feast, coinciding with the grain harvest, or "Weeks/Pentecost" (Shavuoth), when food offerings were brought to Yahweh; and the fall festival, or "Booths" (Succoth), when fruits and other produce were ripe, and whole families camped in "booths" in the fields to complete the joyful harvest at year's end, followed shortly by the onset of the winter rains and the beginning of the new year (Rosh ha-Shanah, followed by Yom Kippur and rites of atonement). It is true that all of these festivals may later have been demythologized to some extent, in keeping with Israel's characteristic historicizing tendencies—i.e., incorporated into the recitation of Yahweh's saving acts in her own history. But their Canaanite origins and connections remained clear to many, especially in early Israel.[31]

Later, in the Monarchy, the Israelite cult was of course more highly centralized and institutionalized by the Jerusalem priesthood. But, as we have seen, the official version of Israelite religion enshrined in the Hebrew Bible produced by these circles is sometimes more pious fiction than fact. The archaeological discoveries we have surveyed make it indisputably clear that local shrines and even rival temples continued in use after Solomon, and that Baᶜal and Asherah were commonly worshipped down to the very end of the Monarchy. Monotheistic Judaism was a product of the Exile, not earlier, as both the Bible itself and Jewish tradition strongly suggest. Until then, the ancient fertility cults of Canaan held powerful sway; indeed, all the old gods and goddesses of Canaan survived into Persian and Phoenician times, finally reincarnated in the familiar deities of Greece and Rome: El is Kronos, Baᶜal is Zeus, Asherah is Aphrodite, ᶜAnat is Athena, and so on.[32]

The similarities of Israelite religion to the religions of greater Canaan have long been known, and indeed are assumed by one strand of the tradition in the Hebrew Bible. But the degree of affinity and of actual continuity with Canaan have been minimized by scholars, both Jewish and Christian, to emphasize the uniqueness of ancient Israel. Recent archaeological discoveries redress the balance by showing that in terms of material culture and the behavior it reflects, there was very little distinction between Canaanite and Israelite religion, at least in practice. The rituals were virtually the same, even if one assumes that Israel's Yahwistic theology was an innovation—and that is not always evident.[33]

CONCLUSION

An agreement concerning the proper relation of archaeology to Biblical studies requires a serious and objective understanding of what the Bible is and what it is not. In these chapters I have attempted to demonstrate how textual facts, artifacts, and ecofacts combine to illuminate the world of the Bible, and how archaeology contributes by creating a setting in which the Bible may become more credible for many. Ultimately, however, the Bible is not history, but rather an account of God's miraculous intervention in human history. Whether one accepts this premise, the Bible's central claim is a personal, not a scholarly matter. It is a choice that may be based on social conditioning, personal predilection, or individual experience—but it is not a rational choice based on irrefutable proof of specific historical events.

In my judgment, there is little authentic religion or piety in the populist notion of "Biblical archaeology." At its best—in the work of conscientious and sincere researchers—it is too Bibliocentric to offer an adequate perspective on ancient oriental history and religion in general. At its worst, it is hypocritical. Some of its staunchest supporters are not themselves believers—in the Biblical sense— but only Bibliophiles. In this respect, secular historians and archaeologists are more honest, and in the long run their research may be truer to the spirit of the Bible. In any case, the distortions rampant in Biblical archaeology are perversions both of Biblical faith and of archaeology as serious, scholarly inquiry.

Archaeology never sought to make a convert of a nonbeliever, nor surely ever did so. It could even be argued that the partial rationale offered by archaeology provides the very antithesis of faith for those who consider such justifications an *apologia pro fidei sua*. Nothing could be clearer evidence of the modern lack of faith than our exaggerated expectations and demands for archaeological "proof." It is perhaps misleading to insist that we have asked too much of archaeology. Rather, we have been asking the wrong questions. (Ironically, much of the public's fascination with recent excavations may be due to the fact that archaeology has become a secular surrogate for religion, a nostalgic search for history and a sense of identity that formerly derived from religion. This explanation certainly is consistent with the archaeological craze in Israel today, an increasingly secular society in which pursuing the lastest find is a national pastime.)

In Richard M. Weaver's book *The Ethics of Rhetoric*, a treatment of Greek philosophy, he points out that

> it is a matter of curious interest that a warning against literal reading occurs at an early stage of the *Phaedrus*. Here in the opening pages, appearing as if to set the key of the theme, comes an allusion to the myth of Boreas and Oreithyia. . . . Does Socrates believe that this tale is really true? Or is he in favor of a scientific explanation of what the myth alleges? . . . The answer of Socrates is that many tales are open to this kind of rationalization, but that the result is tedious and actually irrelevant. It is irrelevant because our chief concern is with the nature of the man, and it is beside the point to probe into such matters while we are yet ignorant of ourselves. The scientific criticism of Greek mythology, which may be likened to the scientific criticism of the myths of the Bible in our own day, produces at best "a boorish sort of wisdom." It is a limitation to suppose that the truth of the story lies in its historicity. The "boorish sort of wisdom" seeks to supplant poetic allegation with fact, just as an archaeologist might look for the foundations of the Garden of Eden. But while this sort of search goes on the truth flies off, on wings of imagination, and is not recoverable until the searcher attains a higher level of pursuit.[1]

In the same way, a mechanical, literalistic reading of the Bible, as though it were mere history, misses the point.

It is my purpose and hope to point toward a middle way that is both more realistic and more conducive to a real understanding of what happened in history, and what it can mean to us today.[2] The new archaeology can, in my view, surpass the task of mere verification—valuable though that may be—and in so doing lay the foundation for an altogether new approach to the study of Israelite religion.

The first key to this truly radical approach lies in the capacity of modern archaeology to document the "ecology of change": that is, its potential—only beginning to be realized—to reconstruct the cultural and material setting for historical events. In this way Israel's emergence in Canaan can be elucidated as a distinctive social and economic reality, rather than being observed as merely a religious movement or assumed to be supernatural. I quote Norman Gottwald's recent *Tribes of Yahweh*, whose approach is so congenial to many modern archaeologists:

Yahweh and "his" people Israel must be demystified, deromanticized, dedogmatized and deidolized. Only as we carry through this sociological demythologization of Yahwistic faith, and of its Jewish and Christian derivatives, will those of us who have been formed and nurtured by those curiously ambiguous Jewish and Christian symbols be able to align heart and head, to combine theory and practice.[3]

Second, modern archaeology begins to give Israelite "ethnicity" a real definition, both in terms of distinctive material culture traits and in terms of the patterns of behavior they reflect. Religious practice is, of course, significant among these traits and patterns. In this area, archaeological research is only in its infancy, but a promising beginning has been made in the first surveys of early Israelite villages, as discussed in this book.

Yet the limitations of inquiry by means of archaeological investigation alone must be kept constantly in mind. As an illustration, and a concluding example, imagine that a certain Canaanite site in central Palestine could be positively identified as one of the principal cities said by the Book of Joshua to have been destroyed by the incoming Israelites. Excavations there reveal a heavy destruction layer that dates indisputably to ca. 1200 B.C. Immediately above these ruins there is a new occupation level, entirely different in its style of houses and pottery, burial customs, and other aspects of material culture—clear evidence of the appearance of a new ethnic group. Finally, imagine that excavations are crowned by the discovery of a victory stela in this newly established town, inscribed in early Hebrew, documenting in detail the conquest of the site and specifically naming Joshua and the Israelites.

Is this concrete evidence of the historicity of the Book of Joshua? Is this the long-sought proof that "the Bible is true"? Not at all. The significant message of the Bible is not, after all, that the Israelites *took* Canaan by military might. Its essential claim is that that God miraculously *gave* them the land of Canaan as an unforgettable sign that he had chosen Israel as his own special people. That is a theological claim—not a documentation of events, but an interpretation of them.

We may or may not someday be able to demonstrate that all the events recorded in the Bible did or did not take place, but in the end it matters very little. Religious consciousness leaps beyond event to meaning. Claims for truth of a higher order are simply not amenable to historical or archaeological investigation; nor do they benefit by historical or archaeological confirmation. They are matters of faith.

Notes

Frequently cited sources are identified by the following abbreviations:

BA   *Biblical Archaeologist*
BAR   *Biblical Archaeology Review*
BASOR   *Bulletin of the American Schools of Oriental Research*
EAEHL   *Encyclopedia of Archaeological Excavations in the Holy Land*, edited by B.
         Mazar and E. Stern. 4 vols. Jerusalem: Massada Press, 1975–78.
IEJ   *Israel Exploration Journal*

Chapter 1

1. On the literary types of the Hebrew Bible, see such standard recent handbooks as D. A. Knight and G. M. Tucker, *The Hebrew Bible and Its Modern Interpreters* (Chico, Calif.: Scholars Press, 1985).

2. See, for instance, the eloquent statements of B. W. Anderson, in *Rediscovering the Bible* (New York: Association Press, 1951); G. E. Wright and R. H. Fuller, *The Book of the Acts of God* (New York: Doubleday, 1957).

3. For general orientation to the problems of writing a history of ancient Israel, see the essays in *Israelite and Judaean History*, edited by J. H. Hayes and J. M. Miller (Philadelphia: Westminster Press, 1977); specifically on archaeology and the Patriarchs, see my essay, "The Patriarchal Traditions: Palestine in the Second Millennium B.C.E.: The Archaeological Picture," pp. 70–120. See also J. M. Miller, *The Old Testament and the Historian* (Philadelphia: Fortress Press, 1976).

4. On the social world of the prophets, see R. R. Wilson, *Prophecy and Society in Ancient Israel* (Philadelphia: Fortress Press, 1980); and also M. Silver, *Prophets and Markets: The Political Economy of Ancient Israel* (Boston: Kluwer-Nijhott Publishers, 1983).

5. On the problems of literary, form, and other methods of critical analysis, in general see notes 1 and 3 above; also, Fortress Press in Philadelphia publishes an excellent, nontechnical series entitled Guides to Biblical Scholarship, in which several volumes deal with modern critical methods in the study of the Hebrew Bible. On the transmission of the Biblical text, see B. J. Roberts, *The Old Testament Text and Versions* (Cardiff: University of Wales Press, 1951).

6. See J. M. Miller's essay in Miller and Hayes, *Israelite and Judaean History*.

7. See n. 5.

8. J. Barr's *The Bible in the Modern World* (New York: Harper & Row, 1973) gives an eminently readable account of these controversies from a Liberal Christian perspective.

9. Although it is beyond the scope of this book, I call attention to the considerable literature on hermeneutics and epistemology (theories of interpretation and knowledge) in both Biblical studies and archaeological theory today. The fundamental question has to do with how we can know *anything* with certainty about the past through either texts or artifacts.

10. This recycling is a part of what archaeologists call "cultural formation processes," or how the debris found by archaeologists in a typical mound forms and is transformed over time. See, for instance, M. B. Schiffer, *Formation Processes of the Archaeological Record* (Albuquerque: University of New Mexico, 1987).

11. For a brief history and critique of "Biblical archaeology," see my chapter in Knight and Tucker, pp. 31–74, summarizing several earlier published treatments. A general history of American Syro-Palestinian and Biblical archaeology has yet to be written, but the history of one of the principal institutions, the American Schools of Oriental Research, will be found in P. J. King, *American Archaeology in the Middle East* (Philadelphia: American Schools of Oriental Research, 1983). An earlier essay by G. E. Wright is still useful, "The Phenomenon of American Archaeology in the Near East," in *Near Eastern Archaeology in the Twentieth Century*, edited by J. A. Sanders (Garden City, New York: Doubleday, 1970), pp. 3–40.

12. A. Alt, "Edward Robinson and the Historical Geography of Palestine," *Journal of Biblical Literature* 58 (1939): 374. For more on Robinson, see Wright (n. 11), pp. 3–8.

13. See *Memoirs of the American Palestine Exploration Society*, Vol. 1 (1971).

14. On the history of ASOR, see P. J. King (n. 11).

15. For an assessment of Albright and his achievement, see G. E. Wright (n. 11), pp. 23–28; P. J. King (n. 11), pp. 52–90, 229–35, *et passim*. A biography of Albright (although unfortunately not critical) has been prepared by Leona Running, under the title *William Foxwell Albright: A Twentieth Century Genius* (New York: Two Continents Publishing Group, 1975).

16. J. W. Newton, in W. W. Prescott, *The Spade and the Bible: Archaeology Supports the Old Book* (New York: Fleming H. Revell, 1933), p. 65.

17. W. F. Albright, *The Archaeology of Palestine and the Bible* (Cambridge, Mass., American Schools of Oriental Research, 1974; re-issue of the 1935 version), pp. 137, 138.

18. G. E. Wright, *God Who Acts: Biblical Theology as Recital* (London: SCM Press, 1952), pp. 126, 127. For a critique of Wright's coupling of theology and archaeology, see my article, "Biblical Theology and Biblical Archaeology: An Appreciation of G. Ernest Wright," *Harvard Theological Review* 73 (1980): 1–15; and my chapter in Knight and Tucker (n. 11).

19. See my chapter in Knight and Tucker (n. 11), pp. 55, 56, and references there.

20. G. E. Wright, *Biblical Archaeology* (Philadelphia: Westminster Press, 1957), p. 17.

21. G. E. Wright, "Biblical Archaeology Today," in *New Directions in Biblical Archaeology*, edited by D. N. Freeman and J. Greenfield (Garden City, New York: Doubleday, 1969), pp. 149–65.

22. For further discussion, see my chapter in Knight and Tucker.

23. For further discussion, see my chapter in Knight and Tucker, pp. 57–59.

24. See my chapter in Knight and Tucker (above, n. 11); and W. G. Dever, "Retrospects and Prospects in Biblical and Syro-Palestinian Archaeology," *BA* 45 (1982): 103–7.

25. See my treatment referred to in n. 3 above, with exhaustive references to the literature up until 1976. Little has changed since then with the accumulation of new data.

26. D. N. Freedman, as reported by the editor, Hershel Shanks, in *BAR* 11, no. 1 (1985): 6.

27. See my résumé cited in n. 11 above; and "The Impact of the 'New Archaeology' on Syro-Palestinian Archaeology," *BASOR* 242 (1980): 15–29; "Archaeological Method in Israel: A Continuing Revolution," *BA* 43 (1980): 41–48.

28. See the works cited in nn. 24, 27.

29. M. S. Smith, "The Present State of Old Testament Studies," *Journal of Biblical Literature* 88 (1969): 34.

30. See W. G. Dever et al., "Further Excavations at Gezer, 1967–71," *BA* 24 (1971): 112-17.

31. On the latest evidence from Lachish, see popular accounts in D. Ussishkin, "Answers at Lachish," *BAR* 5, no. 6 (1979): 16–39; "News from the Field: Defensive Judean Counter-ramp Found at Lachish in 1983 Season," *BAR* 10, no. 2 (1984): 66–73 (also H. Shanks, "Destruction of Judean Fortress Portrayed in Dramatic Eighth-Century B.C. Pictures," same issue, 48–65). For a more technical preliminary report, see D. Ussishkin, "Excavations at Tel Lachish, 1973–1977," *Tel Aviv* 5 (1978): 1–97. A new, lavishly illustrated treatment of the famous Lachish reliefs is Ussishkin et al., *The Conquest of Lachish by Sennacherib* (Tel Aviv: Institute of Archaeology, 1982).

32. N. K. Gottwald, *The Tribes of Yahweh: A Sociology of the Religion of Liberated Israel, 1250–1050 B.C.E.* (Maryknoll, New York: Orbis Books, 1979), p. xxv.

Chapter 2

1. See B. W. Anderson, *Rediscovering the Bible* (New York: Association Press, 1951), pp. 23–87; G. E. Wright, *God Who Acts: Biblical Theology as Recital* (London: SCM Press, 1952).

2. See chapter 1, nn. 1, 3.

3. See J. M. Miller, "The Israelite Occupation of Canaan," in *Israelite and Judean History*, edited by J. H. Hayes and J. M. Miller (Philadelphia: Westminster Press, 1977), pp. 213–84. Also I. Finkelstein, *The Archaeology of the Israelite Settlement* (Jerusalem: Israel Exploration Society, 1988).

4. On the Amarna Letters, see n. 5, and nn. 19, 20.

5. See *Ancient Near Eastern Texts Relating to the Old Testament*, edited by J. B. Pritchard (Princeton: Princeton University Press, 1955), pp. 376–78.

6. For illustrations, see J. B. Pritchard, *The Ancient Near East in Pictures* (Princeton: Princeton University Press, 1954). The standard work on the Philistines is now Trude Dothan, *The Philistines and Their Material Culture* (Jerusalem: Israel Exploration Society, 1982).

7. See further, with full references, J. M. Miller (n. 3), pp. 245–52.

8. On Tell Beit Mirsim, see conveniently *EAEHL* 1, pp. 171–78.; on Rabûd, see *EAEHL* 4: p. 995.

9. On the older Lachish excavations, see conveniently *EAEHL* 3, pp. 735–53. On the renewed Israeli excavations at Lachish, see D. Ussishkin, "Excavations at Tel Lachish 1978–1983: Second Preliminary Report," *Tel Aviv* 10 (1983): 97–175.

10. See K. M. Kenyon, *Digging Up Jericho* (London: Ernest Benn Ltd., 1957), pp. 167–72, 256–63; *EAEHL* 2, pp. 550–64.

11. On ʿAi, see J. A. Callaway, "Excavating at ʿAi (Et-Tell), 1964–1972," *BA* 39 (1976): 18–30; *EAEHL* 1, pp. 37–52.

12. See J. B. Pritchard, *Gibeon, Where the Sun Stood Still* (Princeton: Princeton University Press, 1962), pp. 30–34, 157–59; *EAEHL* 2, pp. 446–50.

13. See Yadin, *Hazor, The Rediscovery of a Great Citadel of the Bible* (London: Weidenfeld and Nicolson, 1975), pp. 144, 145, 249–57; *EAEHL* 2, pp. 474–95.

14. The discussion on early Israelite technology may be brought up to date by consulting N. K. Gottwald, *The Tribes of Yahweh: A Sociology of the Religion of Liberated Israel, 1250–1050 B.C.E.* (Maryknoll, New Jersey: Orbis Books, 1979), pp. 650–63, and references there; L. E. Stager, "The Archaeology of the Family in Ancient Israel," *BASOR* 260 (1985): 1–35, and references there; cf. n. 30.

15. See G. E. Wright, *Biblical Archaeology* (Philadelphia: Westminster Press, 1957), pp. 69–84; esp. p. 83.

16. John Bright, *A History of Israel* (Philadelphia: Westminster Press, 1959), pp. 117–20, 126, 127.

17. P. W. Lapp, "The Conquest of Palestine in the Light of Archaeology," *Concordia Theological Monthly* 38 (1967): 283–300.

18. Aharoni's major work is in Hebrew, but see "New Aspects of the Israelite Occupation in the North," in *Near Eastern Archaeology in the Twentieth Century*, edited by J. A. Sanders (Garden City, New York: Doubleday, 1970), pp. 254–65; "Nothing Early and Nothing Late: Rewriting Israel's Conquest," BA 39 (1976): 55–76.

19. On the "German school," see especially the convenient summary in M. Weippert's *The Settlement of the Israelite Tribes in Palestine: A Critical Survey of Recent Debate* (London: SCM Press, 1971); and cf. an American critique in J. Bright, *Early Israel in Recent History Writing* (Chicago: Alec R. Allenson, 1956).

20. For Mendenhall's early views, see "The Hebrew Conquest of Palestine," BA 25 (1962): 66–87 (the quotation here is from p. 73); and cf. *The Tenth Generation: The Origins of the Biblical Tradition* (Baltimore: The Johns Hopkins University Press, 1973).

21. See N. K. Gottwald (n. 14), p. xxv.

22. See the older treatments of Lapp (n. 17) and Miller (n. 3), as well as Gottwald (n. 14). Useful surveys of the older literature will also be found in several chapters in *Symposia Celebrating the Seventy-fifth Anniversary of the Founding of the American Schools of Oriental Research (1900–1975)* edited by F. M. Cross (Cambridge: American Schools of Oriental Research, 1979); and in M. Weippert (n. 19). An up-to-date treatment of some aspects of the emergence of early Israel, from an archaeological perspective, will be found in W. G. Dever, "The Contribution of Archaeology to the Study of Canaanite and Early Israelite Religion," in *Ancient Israelite Religion: Essays in Honor of Frank Moore Cross*, edited by P. D. Miller, Jr., Paul D. Hanson, and S. Dean McBride (Philadelphia: Fortress Press, 1987), pp. 209–47. See also my forthcoming article "The Israelite Settlement" in the *Anchor Bible Dictionary*; and R. B. Coote and K. W. Whitelam, *The Emergence of Israel in Historical Perspective* (Sheffield: Almond Press, 1987).

23. See J. A. Callaway (n. 11); and "A Visit With Ahilud," BAR 9, no. 5 (1983): 42–53; Z. Zevit, "The Problem of ʿAi," BAR 11, no. 2 (1985): 58–69 and references there.

24. See n. 23.

25. On Tel Masos, the only convenient preliminary reports in English are in the Israeli journal *Tel Aviv* 2 (1975) and 4 (1977).

26. See M. Kochavi, "An Ostracon of the Period of the Judges from ʿIzbet

Ṣarṭah," *Tel Aviv* 4 (1977); and a popular account in A. Demsky and M. Kochavi, "An Alphabet from the Days of the Judges," *BAR* 4, no. 3 (1978): 23–30. A much fuller treatment, in Hebrew, is the doctoral dissertation of Israel Finkelstein, "The ʿIzbet Sartah Excavations and the Israelite Settlement in the Hill Country" (Tel Aviv: Tel Aviv University, 1983), published in English as *ʿIzbet Ṣarṭah: An Early Iron Age Site Near Rosh Haʿayin, Israel* (Oxford: British Archaeological Reports, International Series, 1985).

27. See A. Mazar, "Giloh: An Early Israelite Settlement Site Near Jerusalem," *IEJ* 31 (1981): 1–36.

28. For a convenient, though still preliminary, treatment of the new survey data, see my article cited above (n. 22). See also L. E. Stager (n. 14); Finkelstein's survey of the area north and west of Jerusalem (n. 26); on the lower Galillee, Z. Gal's Hebrew dissertation, "The Lower Galilee in the Iron Age" (Tel Aviv University, 1982). The survey work of A. Zertal in the northern part of the West Bank is largely unpublished, but see his Hebrew dissertation, "The Settlement of the Tribes of Israel in the Manasseh Region" (Tel Aviv University, 1987).

29. See my programmatic treatment cited above (n. 22).

30. See n. 14. See also J. A. Callaway, "A New Perspective on the Hill Country Settlement of Canaan in Iron Age I," in the Olga Tufnell Festschrift, *Palestine in the Bronze and Iron Ages*, edited by J. Tubb (London: Institute of Archaeology, 1986), pp. 31–49. Two related recent studies view Israelite origins largely in terms of an emergent peasant agricultural economy and society in the highlands: D. L. Hopkins, *The Highlands of Canaan: Agricultural Life in the Early Iron Age* (Sheffield: Almond Press, 1985); and R. B. Coote and K. W. Whitelam, *The Emergence of Israel in Historical Perspective* (Sheffield: Almond Press, 1987). See also N. P. Lemche, *Early Israel: Anthropological and Historical Studies of the Israelite Society Before the Monarchy* (Leiden: E. J. Brill, 1985).

31. See P. J. Ackroyd's essay in Knight and Tucker (See chapter 1, n. 1), pp. 300–5, and references there.

Chapter 3

1. For the latest discussion and full references, see J. A. Soggin, "The Davidic-Solomonic Kingdom," in *Israelite and Judean History*, edited by J. H. Hayes and J. M. Miller (Philadelphia: Westminster Press, 1977), pp. 320–80.

2. For convenient summaries and illustrations on all the following sites in this chapter, see the respective entires in *EAEHL* 1–4. On Dan, see *EAEHL* 1, pp. 316–20; A. Biran, "Tell Dan Five Years Later," *BA* 43 (1980): 168–82; J. C. H. Laughlin, "The Remarkable Discoveries at Tel Dan," *BAR* 7, no. 5 (1981): 20–36.

3. See Y. Yadin, *Hazor, The Rediscovery of a Great Citadel of the Bible* (London: Weidenfeld and Nicolson, 1975), pp. 187–99; *EAEHL* 2, pp. 447–95.

4. See Yadin, "Megiddo of the Kings of Israel," *BA* 33 (1970): 66–96; Hazor (n. 3), pp. 207–31; *EAEHL* 2, pp. 848–55.

5. See P. W. Lapp, "Taanach by the Waters of Megiddo," *BA* 30 (1967): 2–27; A. E. Glock, *EAEHL* 4, pp. 1139–47.

6. See R. deVaux, *EAEHL* 2, pp. 395–404.

7. On Shechem, see G. E. Wright, *Shechem: The Biography of a Biblical City* (New York: McGraw-Hill, 1965), pp. 144–45; W. G. Dever, "The MB IIC Stratification of the Northwest Gate Area at Shechem," *BASOR* 216 (1974): 44; G. E. Wright, *EAEHL* 4, pp. 1083–94.

8. On Samaria, see G. E. Wright, "Israelite Samaria and Iron Age Chronology," *BASOR* 155 (1959): 20–21.

9. On Gibeon, see J. B. Pritchard, "Industry and Trade at Biblical Gibeon," *BA* 23 (1960): 23–29; *EAEHL* 2, pp. 446–50.

10. On Gibeah, see P. W. Lapp, Tell el-Fûl," *BA* 28 (1965): 2–10; L. A. Sinclair, "Gibeah," *EAEHL* 2, pp. 444–46; N. L. Lapp, et al., *The Third Campaign at Tell el-Fûl The Excavations of 1964* (Cambridge: American Schools of Oriental Research, 1981).

11. A convenient source of information about recent excavations in Jerusalem is *Jerusalem Revealed: Archaeology in the Holy City,* 1968–1974, edited by Y. Yadin (Jerusalem: Israel Exploration Society, 1975); see also Y. Shiloh, "The City of David Archaeological Project: The Third Season, 1980," *BA* 44 (1981): 161–70; for more recent information see also Y. Shiloh, *Excavations at the City of David* (Jerusalem: Institute of Archaeology, 1984).

12. On Gezer, see W. G. Dever, et al., "Further Excavations at Gezer, 1967–71, *BA* 34 (1971): 94–132; "Gezer, Tell," *EAEHL* 2, pp. 428–43; "Gezer Revisited: New Excavations of the Solomonic and Assyrian Period Defenses," *BA* 47 (1984): 206–18.

13. On Lachish, see D. Ussishkin, "Excavations at Tel Lachish, 1973–1977," *Tel Aviv* 5 (1978): 116–26, 147–54; *EAEHL* 3, pp. 735–52; Y. Aharoni, *Investigations at Lachish: The Sanctuary and the Residency (Lachish V)* (Tel Aviv: Institute of Archaeology, 1975), pp. 3–11, 26–32.

14. On Beersheba, see Y. Aharoni, *Beer-Sheba I: Excavations at Tel Beer-Sheba, 1969–71 Seasons* (Tel Aviv: Institute of Archaeology, 1973), pp. 5–67; *EAEHL* 1, pp. 160–68; cf. Z. Herzog, "Beer-Sheba of the Patriarchs," *BAR* 6, no. 6 (1980): 12–28.

15. On Arad, see Y. Aharoni, "Arad: Its Inscriptions and Temple," *BA* 31 (1968): 2–32; *EAEHL* 1, pp. 82–89; Z. Herzog et al., "The Israelite Fortress at Arad," *BASOR* 254 (1984): 1–34.

16. On the Negev forts, see R. Cohen, "The Iron Age Fortresses in the Central Negev," *BASOR* 236 (1979): 61–79.

17. On Ezion-geber, see N. Glueck, *EAEHL* 3, pp. 713–17.

18. On Kadesh Barnea, see C. Meyers, "Kadesh Barnea: Judah's Last Outpost," *BA* 39 (1976): 145–51; *EAEHL* 3, 697, 698.

19. See Y. Shiloh, "The Four-Room House: Its Situation and Function in the Israelite City," *IEJ* 20 (1970): 180–90; but cf. A. Mazar, "Giloh: An Early Israelite Settlement Site Near Jerusalem," *IEJ* 31 (1981): 6–11, on the identification as "Israelite"; see also L. E. Stager, "The Archaeology of the Family in Early Israel," *BASOR* 260 (1985): pp. 11–17.

20. On these city gates, see nn. 3, 4, 12; see also K. W. Whitelam, "The Symbols of Power: Aspects of Royal Propaganda in the United Monarchy," *BA* 49 (1986): 166–73.

21. See n. 4; and D. Ussishkin, "King Solomon's Palaces," *BA* 36 (1973): 78–105.

22. See n. 12.

23. On the Solomonic Temple, see the older treatment of G. E. Wright in *Biblical Archaeology* (Philadelphia: Westminster, 1957), pp. 129–145. See also D. Ussishkin, "King Solomon's Palace and Building 1723 in Megiddo," *IEJ* 16 (1966): pp. 174–86; W. G. Dever (n. 7); C. L. Meyers, "The Elusive Temple," *BA* 45 (1982): 33–41; V. Fritz, "What Can Archaeology Tell Us About Solomon's Temple?" *BAR* 8, no. 4 (1987): 38–49.

24. On the excavations of Y. Shiloh in the City of David, see n. 11.

Chapter 4

1. See my chapter in the F. M. Cross *Festschrift* (1987), "The Contribution of Archaeology to the Study of Canaanite and Early Israelite Religion" (chapter 2, n. 22); and also a programmatic essay, "Material Remains and the Cult in Ancient Israel: An Essay in Archaeological Systematics," in *The Word of the Lord Goes Forth: Essays in Honor of David Noel Freedman on His Sixtieth Birthday*, edited by C. L. Meyers and M. O'Conner (Winona Lake, Indiana: Eisenbrauns, 1983), pp. 571–87. Full references to the literature on our topic will be found in these works. See also P. D. Miller, "Israelite Religion," in *The Hebrew Bible and Its Modern Interpreters*, edited by D. A. Knight and G. M. Tucker (Chico, California: Scholars Press, 1985), pp. 201–37.

2. The latest summaries on the archaeology of Israel's neighbors will be found in several chapters in *Biblical Archaeology Today: Proceedings of the International Congress on Biblical Archaeology*, edited by J. Amitai (Jerusalem: Israel Exploration Society, 1985; see also J. A. Sauer, "Transjordan in the Bronze and Iron Ages: A Critique of Glueck's Synthesis," *BASOR* 263 (1986): 1–26. Excellent treat-

ments of the textual and historical evidence are contained in D. J. Wiseman, *Peoples of Old Testament Times* (Oxford: Clarendon Press, 1973). For the archaeology of Jordan in more detail, see *Studies in the History and Archaeology of Jordan*, edited by A. Hadidi, Vol. 1 (London: Oxford 1982).

3. In the foregoing comments, for purposes of argumentation I may have overstated the notion that the Bible is priestly—"elitist"—and idealized in its picture of Israelite religion. Some portions of the Hebrew Bible do portray popular religion—whether approved or not—such as certain narratives in Judges, in much of the Deuteronomistic material, in several of the Prophets, and in the miscellaneous collection known as the "Writings," especially Job. My portrait of a late, elitist document is truer of the Pentateuch than of the Hebrew Bible as a whole. The portrait will be somewhat better balanced below.

4. See references in chapter 1, nn. 1, 3, 5.

5. The literature on "Biblical Theology" is vast, but for general orientation and references see C. F. Hasel, *Old Testament Theology: Basic Issues in the Current Debate* (Grand Rapids: Wm. B. Erdmans, 1975). See also the earlier critique in B. S. Childs, *Biblical Theology in Crisis* (Philadelphia: Westminster Press, 1970); and the latest survey in G. W. Coats, "Theology of the Hebrew Bible," in *The Hebrew Bible and Its Modern Interpreters*, edited by D. A. Knight and G. M. Tucker (Chico, California: Scholars Press, 1985), pp. 239–62.

6. For survey and critique of recent literature, see P. D. Miller, "Israelite Religion," in Knight and Tucker (n. 5), pp. 201–37; and several chapters in *Ancient Israelite Religion* (cited in chapter 2, n. 22).

7. See my more extended treatments, cited in n. 1.

8. See Norman C. Habel, *Yahweh Versus Ba*ᶜ*al: A Conflict of Religious Cultures* (New York: Bookman Associates for Concordia Theological Seminary [St. Louis] 1964).

9. See the preliminary report in A. Mazar, "The 'Bull Site': An Iron Age I Open Cult Place," *BASOR* 247 (1982): 27–42; "Bronze Bull Found in Israelite 'High Place' from the Time of the Judges," *BAR* 9, no. 5 (1983): 34–40.

10. For a preliminary study (to be used with caution, however), see A. Zertal, "Has Joshua's Altar Been Found on Mt. Ebal?," *BAR* 11, no. 1 (1985): 26–45; and the contrasting interpretation of A. Kempinski, "Joshua's Altar: An Iron Age Watchtower," *BAR* 12, no. 1 (1986): 42–49.

11. See A. Biran, "Tell Dan Five Years Later," *BA* 43 (1980): 168–82; "An Israelite Horned Altar at Dan," *BA* 37 (1974): 106, 107; L. E. Stager and S. R. Wolff, "Production and Commerce in Temple Courtyards: An Olive Press in the Sacred Precinct at Tel Dan," *BASOR* 243 (1981): 95–102. This and some of the following tenth century B.C. shrines are treated in Y. Shilah, "Iron Age Sanctuaries and Cult Elements in Palestine," in *Symposia Celebrating the Seventy-*

fifth Anniversary of the American Schools of Oriental Research (1900–1975), edited by F. M. Cross (Cambridge: American Schools of Oriental Research, 1979), pp. 147–57.

12. G. Loud, *Megiddo*, Vol. 2 (Chicago: University of Chicago, 1948), pp. 45, 46, figs. 100, 101, 102.

13. See P. W. Lapp, "Taanach by the Waters of Megiddo," *BA* 30 (1967): 2–27; A. E. Glock, *EAEHL* 4, pp. 1139–47. On the oil press, see Stager and Wolff (n. 11).

14. For convenient references to the cult of Asherah, see W. G. Dever, "Asherah, Consort of Yahweh? New Evidence from Kuntillet ʿAjrûd," *BASOR* 255 (1984): 21–37.

15. See n. 11.

16. See Y. Aharoni, *Lachish: The Sanctuary and the Residency (Lachish V)* (Tel Aviv: Institute of Archaeology, 1975), pp. 26–32; *EAEHL* 3, pp. 747–49.

17. On the Arad temple, see Y. Aharoni, "Arad: Its Inscriptions and Temple," *BA* 31 (1968): 1–32; *EAEHL* 1, pp. 82–88; Z. Herzog et al., "The Israelite Fortress at Arad," *BASOR* 254 (1984): 1–34.

18. For preliminary reports, see Z. Meshel, "Did Yahweh Have a Consort? The New Religious Inscriptions from Sinai," *BAR* 5, no. 1 (1979): 24–34. For an art-historical treatment, which takes a minimalist approach, see P. Beck, "The Drawings from Ḥorvat Teiman (Kuntillet ʿAjrud)," *Tel Aviv* 9 (1982): 3–86; contrast my approach (n. 14), which seeks to identify the goddess "Asherah" in these drawings.

19. Cf. nn. 14, 18.

20. Cf. nn. 14, 18.

21. See the original publication in W. G. Dever, "Iron Age Epigraphic Material from the Area of Khirbet el-Kôm," *Hebrew Union College Annual* 40–41 (1970): 139–204; and cf. the more recent discussions, as summarized in Z. Zevit, "The Khirbet el-Qôm Inscription Mentioning a Goddess," *BASOR* 255 (1984): 39–47.

22. On the Dan, Megiddo, and Lachish, altars, see nn. 11, 12, 16; for the Beersheba altar, see Y. Aharoni, "The Horned Altar of Beer-sheba," *BA* 37 (1974): 2–6.

23. See M. D. Fowler, "Excavated Incense Burners," *BA* 47 (1984): 183–86; C. L. Meyers, *The Tabernacle Menorah: A Synthetic Study of a Symbol from the Biblical Cult* (Missoula, Montana: Scholars Press, 1976); and L. F. Derries, "Cult Stands: A Bewildering Variety of Shapes and Sizes," *BAR* 8, no. 4 (1987): 26–37.

24. See A. Chambon, *Tell el-Farʿah I. L'Age du fer* (Paris: Éditions Recherche sur les Civilisations, 1984), 66. Other examples will be found in S. S. Weinberg, "A Moabite Shrine Group," *Muse* 12 (1978): 30–48.

25. There is no readily accessible study of the *kernoi*, but see examples and

references in A. Mazar, *Excavations at Tell Qasile*, Part 1, *The Philistine Sanctuary: Architecture and Cult Objects* (Jerusalem: Institute of Archaeology, 1980).

26. See references and discussions cited in n. 14.

27. K. M. Kenyon, *Jerusalem: Excavating 3000 Years of History* (London: McGraw-Hill, 1967), pp. 84–104, figs. 8–10.

28. Again, there are no convenient, nontechnical studies of Israelite seals, except older works such as A. Reifenberg, *Ancient Hebrew Seals* (London: East and West Library, 1948).

29. On the ivories, see R. D. Barnett, *Ancient Ivories in the Middle East and Adjacent Countries* (Jerusalem: Institute of Archaeology, 1982).

30. See W. G. Dever, "Biblical Theology and Biblical Archaeology: An Appreciation of G. Ernest Wright," *Harvard Theological Review* 73 (1980): 1–15, and references there. For the publication of the temple, see G. E. Wright, *Shechem: The Biography of a Biblical City* (New York: McGraw-Hill, 1965), pp. 123–138.

31. On ancient Israelite festivals, see H. J. Kraus, *Worship in Israel: A Cultic History of the Old Testament* (Richmond: John Knox Press, 1966), pp. 26–92; and also R. de Vaux, *Ancient Israel, Its Life and Institutions* (New York: McGraw-Hill, 1961), pp. 481–517.

32. See R. A. Oden, Jr., "The Persistence of Canaanite Religion," *BA* 39 (1976): 31–36.

33. See my forthcoming treatment (n. 1) for details.

Conclusion

1. R. M. Weaver, *The Ethics of Rhetoric* (South Bend: Regnery/Gateway, 1953), pp. 4, 5. I am indebted to my student Jean Clark for referring me to this work.

2. For those wishing to pursue the question of the relation of archaeology to Biblical studies from perspectives somewhat different than those presented here, the following articles are significant: H. D. Lance, "American Biblical Archaeology in Perspective," *BA* 45 (1982): 97–101 (a response to my article cited in n. 24); J. M. Miller, "Approaches to the Bible Through History and Archaeology: Biblical History as a Discipline," *BA* 45 (1982): 211–16; J. A. Sauer, "Syro-Palestinian Archaeology, History, and Biblical Studies," *BA* 45 (1982): 201–9; P. J. King, "The Contribution of Archaeology to Biblical Studies," *Catholic Biblical Quarterly* 45 (1983): 1–16; E. M. Meyers, "The Bible and Archaeology," *BA* 47 (1984): 36–40. These works all reflect a decidedly American point of view. This aspect of archaeological theory and method is much less discussed in Israel; but see Y. Yadin, "Biblical Archaeology Today: The Archaeological As-

pect," in *Biblical Archaeology Today. Proceedings of the International Congress on Biblical Archaeology, Jerusalem, April,* 1984, edited by J. Amitai (Jerusalem: Israel Exploration Society, 1985), pp. 21–27. Useful handbooks are L. J. Hoppe, *What Are They Saying About Biblical Archaeology?* (Ramsey, NJ: Paulist Press, 1984); and, more technical, H. D. Lance, *The Old Testament and the Archaeologist* (Philadelphia: Fortress Press, 1981).

3. N. K. Gottwald, *The Tribes of Yahweh: A Sociology of the Religion of Liberated Israel, 1250–1050 B.C.E.* (Maryknoll, New Jersey: Orbis Books, 1979), p. 708.

Index